INTRODUCTION TO THE SERIES

The Legal Guide for Small Business provides a starting point and path to additional information on each topic. It contains many practical suggestions that are based on legal rules and conditions present in the real world of small business.

The Legal Guide for Small Business describes and interprets the basic laws governing business and commercial relationships relating to business. Your specific needs will dictate the relative importance of each of the topics discussed. A variety of models—corporation, partnership, limited partnership, sole proprietorship and joint venture—provide essential information about starting, owning and operating a small business. The exhibits in Appendix I can be adapted for the particulars of your jurisdiction. Appendix II contains suggestions for additional resources to help you understand your specific issues.

A working manual, *The Legal Guide for Small Business* will give you insight into issues of law and regulation which, as a small business owner, you probably will have to understand. Since the law is complex and ever-changing, be alert to the possibility that decisions or statutes may come along to alter or even negate information contained in this book.

This book will not substitute for legal, accounting or other advice. Consult a professional if you need more specific or detailed advice.

BOOKS IN THE SERIES

- ► **Operating a Really Small Business**
  Betty M. Bivins

- ► **Budgeting: A Primer for Entrepreneurs**
  Terry Dickey

- ► **Getting a Business Loan: Your Step-By-Step Guide**
  Orlando J. Antonini

- ► **Nobody Gets Rich Working for Somebody Else: An Entrepreneur's Guide**
  Roger Fritz

- ► **Marketing Strategies for Small Businesses**
  Richard F. Gerson, Ph.D.

- ► **Financial Basics for Small Business Success**
  James O. Gill

- ► **Extending Credit and Collecting Cash: A Small Business Guide**
  Lynn Harrison

- ► **Avoiding Mistakes in Your New Business**
  David Karlson, Ph.D.

- ► **Buying Your First Franchise: The Least You Need to Know**
  Rebecca Luhn, Ph.D.

- ► **Buying a Business: Tips for the First-Time Buyer**
  Ronald J. McGregor

- ► **Your New Business: A Personal Plan for Success**
  Charles L. Martin, Ph.D.

- ► **Managing the Family Business: A Guide for Success**
  Marshall W. Northington, Ph.D.

- ► **The Legal Guide for Small Business**
  Charles P. Lickson J.D.

THE LEGAL GUIDE
FOR
SMALL BUSINESS

by Charles P. Lickson J.D.

THE
CRISP
SMALL BUSINESS &
ENTREPRENEURSHIP
SERIES

CREDITS

Editor: Beverly Manber

Layout/Design: ExecuStaff

Cover Design: Kathleen Gadway

Library of Congress 93-72970
ISBN-1-56052-266-6

ACKNOWLEDGMENTS

It has been said that it is easier to expand a topic in writing, rather than contract it. Preparing this book has presented that challenge. I had some talented assistance in my daunting task to bring to you the highlights of law for small business.

I thank Susie Gibbs for her invaluable legal research. Herb Hammond, an outstanding intellectual property lawyer from Gardere & Wynne in Dallas, provided an excellent outline on intellectual property law. Christine Chapman, a respected Charlottesville attorney and mediator colleague of mine, was my sounding board and answered many questions.

My colleagues at Mediate-Tech were helpful and patient. Charles Lancaster, my partner, reviewed the book and made valuable contributions to the environmental and dispute resolution sections.

Finally, a special note of thanks to my family. I wrote this book in the midst of an already crowded agenda. Their understanding, willingness to take on some of my usual chores and spiritual support helped me get the job done when, at times, it looked impossible. My oldest daughter, Laura Lickson Stock, was especially generous in allowing me to use my nickname for her as the role model for Laura Little. And I found great inspiration in my other daughter, Karen Lickson Goneau.

CONTENTS

CONTENTS (continued)

CONTENTS (continued)

CONTENTS (continued)

CHAPTER
ONE

GETTING
YOUR
BUSINESS/IDEA
STARTED

WHAT FORM MY BUSINESS SHOULD TAKE

The law does not affect only public figures or notorious characters. It affects each of us in our daily lives—when we make a purchase, start a family, or go to work. To function effectively in our complex society, we must be legally literate.

—The American Bar Association, *You and the Law*

Since this is a book about legal issues and considerations, it will not say much about the kind of planning and thinking needed to launch a business. Suffice it to say that concentrated thought, planning and consideration of a multiplicity of factors must go into the calculations about the decision to start a business. Much has been written on this topic, especially since so many people are considering starting their own businesses, as corporations continue to downsize.[1]

Assuming that you are either about to launch your big venture or that you are already in business, one of the first questions you need to ask is,

What form should my business take? Form of business means the legal structure of the business enterprise. We will look at four forms of business organizations:

- ► Sole proprietorships
- ► Partnerships
- ► Corporations
- ► Joint ventures

To determine what form your business should take, you must first answer some questions about what your business will do.

- ► A sole proprietorship may be the best form if the business is service-oriented. Carpet cleaning is one example of this type of business.

---

1. See also *Your New Business: A Personal Plan for Success,* Charles L. Martin, Ph.D., Crisp Publications, 1993.

► If you and an associate offer professional or advisory services, a partnership may fit your needs.

► Where products are concerned and much contact is expected with the public, a corporation is probably best for you.

Most people who consider the form their businesses should take are interested in the implications from the practical, convenience, personal liability, potential for financial reward and tax standpoints. Since what the business does is so critical to the form it takes, when you ask what legal form the business should take, you must also answer the question,

What will (does) my business do? The following guidelines for business form relate to what a business does. Keep in mind that since these are generalizations, they may not apply specifically to your situation.

Guidelines for Business Forms

If you are to be engaged in a service business—e.g., accounting, business advisory, consulting, writing or public relations—in which your clients do not usually visit your office, you may be best off with a sole proprietorship.

► If your business has a service component and requires or envisions a special relationship with someone besides you—e.g., another accountant, physician or consultant—and you do not invite the general public to your offices, a partnership may be the best arrangement.

► If you offer a product for sale or expect to invite the public to the business premises, a corporation might be best. This would also be true if you are going to raise funds and will sell shares.

► If you are involved in a very specific project with another person or firm and you wish to maintain your independence, a joint venture may be perfect for you.

You will also want to answer the questions:

- ► How much money will my business need?
- ► Where will funding come from?

The methodology of financing a business is closely connected to the form of organization you use. For example, you cannot sell shares in your company if you choose sole proprietorship. On the other hand, if your start-up capital comes as a loan or a gift, sole proprietorship can work for you.

Since this book is not about venture capital or corporate finance, I will not dwell on the challenges posed by raising capital. However, I will state unequivocally that you should not attempt to launch your business until you have carefully thought out and provided for financing. And, one of the methods of providing for it associated with the form your business takes.

For example:

- ► If your business needs to raise considerable funds on the strength of the business concept—and not necessarily the person running it or owning it—a corporation would probably be the best form. A corporation affords a mechanism—sale of shares—to raise funds.

- ► On the other hand, if two people who go into their own service business each agree to contribute an agreed amount of the start-up capital, partnership sounds like it would be the ideal form.

However, do not launch your business until you have provided for financing. While you may want to do most of the launch planning yourself, an accountant or financial advisor can make a real contribution to the financial relevance of the form of business organization.

Before you make your decision on a legal form of organization, you will want to answer this major personal planning question:

What are my personal long-term goals?

For example:

► If you are forming your business to provide a living and a current source of revenue or for personal satisfaction in the present, sole proprietorship is probably your form of choice.

► If you will be working with one or more persons and you are concerned more about current capability than about what will happen to the business after your death, partnership may be most suitable.

► On the other hand, if you are starting a business that should have a life of its own and last even beyond your own life, a corporation form is indicated.

Among the questions you need to answer and consider about your business and the legal form it will take are the following two.

► What is happening to the business now?

► What do I want to happen to the business in the future?

You should not make a choice on the form of the organization without being clear about all three of these factors.

► What the business will do

► How the business will be financed

► Your personal long term goals

CASE STUDY

Laura Little, Graphic Artist

For several years, Laura had worked as a graphic designer in an advertising agency. She liked the people she worked with and the work she did. However, her job started to look less attractive when she married Larry, they moved into a new home and her commute increased considerably.

After some discussion, Laura and Larry decided they could survive financially for a while without Laura's salary; since the new house had room for a studio, they believed it was the right time for Laura to go out on her own and pursue the requests she had for private work.

Laura decided to call her new business The Laura Little Studio. The next question was, how should she organize the new business?

Although she didn't need rental space, Laura realized that she would need several thousands of dollars in equipment and supplies, and she would have other expenses for such necessities as telephone and promotional materials. Laura's dad offered to assist in financing the venture; several of Laura's colleagues wanted to invest and participate. But Laura and Larry wanted to retain complete independence and control over the business. They decided to finance the studio themselves, using a $10,000 bank loan.

Larry ran the U.S. subsidiary of a British high-technology firm. He asked Randy, his firm's lawyer, for advice on what form of legal organization the studio should take. Randy asked Laura what the business would do. She told him it would be an individualized art and design service. She answered no to his next two questions: Would any product be involved? and Would people frequently visit your studio?

When Randy asked about her financial needs, Laura told him that she and Larry had obtained a personal loan to cover the start-up expenses she anticipated.

Randy asked about Laura's personal goals in the business. Laura wanted an outlet for her talents and abilities; she expected to earn some money to supplement Larry's salary. In answer to Randy's questions about her growth plans for the business, Laura felt she would be satisfied with a small, successful business that would keep her busy half-time.

After considering Laura's plans, motivation and goals, Randy suggested a sole proprietorship. He recommended that Laura register to do business in her community in a protected trade name. Laura paid the filing fee and registered the business at Town Hall, doing business as—also known as d/b/a—The Laura Little Studio. The total cost to register the business was under $100. Laura was in business.

As you can see, a simple legal structure and form suited Laura.

To demonstrate the potential real-life possibilities, we will follow the development of The Laura Little Studio during its growth and legal maturity.

OTHER FACTORS IN BUSINESS START-UP

While questions about business purpose, financial needs and personal goals are essential when you consider the best form for your business, you will also need to weigh a number of other factors. Although these are not discussed in detail here, you should consider them when you make your decision about the legal form of your organization:

▶ Licenses (from official agencies) or permissions (from private or public sources) that need to be obtained before you undertake the proposed business activity. For a restaurant, this might be a health department certificate to operate the business.

▶ Restrictions on the proposed name, because of prior use by others or potential for consumer confusion.

▶ Special regulatory or physical requirements to carry out the business. For a home business, this might include verifying that your location is properly zoned for your business.

► Real estate considerations in the business premises, such as location, traffic rules, parking needs and access by disabled persons.

Consider the activity your business will engage in as you read and think about the appropriate form for your organization. If you put off deciding upon the form, you may make an unexpected choice: If you start your business without making a decision, the law will impose the form it considers best fits, whether you like it or not. For example, if the business involves an individual in business, the law will usually classify it as a sole proprietorship; without an agreement or evidence to the contrary, where two or more parties engage in a business, the law will presume it is meant to be a partnership.

ASK YOURSELF

▶ Describe what your business will do and how many people will be involved.

▶ Identify your business's financial needs and potential source(s) for financing.

▶ Discuss your time frame for organizing your business and your personal long-term goals.

▶ What professional advice and counsel will you require?

CHAPTER TWO

SOLE PROPRIETORSHIPS

WHAT ARE SOLE PROPRIE-TORSHIPS?

Sole proprietorships are the easiest type of business organization to form; their structure—or lack of it—gives you the most freedom. Some commentators refer to this structure as proprietorship. As the term sole proprietorship indicates, if anyone else—other than an employee, consultant or creditor—is involved, the business may be treated as a partnership.

HOW ARE SOLE PROPRIETORSHIPS FORMED?

If you want to operate as a sole proprietorship, simply start to do business. No formal documents, filing or special regulatory compliance is needed to operate as a sole proprietor. The name of the business may have to be filed or protected and cannot interfere with someone else's business or confuse the public, but legal requirements are minimal.

A sample certificate of doing business as a sole proprietor can be found in Appendix I as Exhibit 1.

Good News/Bad News

The good news is that sole proprietors have freedom from control by other associates. Therefore, they retain full independence in decision making and actions. They have few regulatory and governmental rules to comply with, since formation of this model is automatic and does not require attorneys or other advisors to help create it.

Since there is virtually no difference between the business and its owner, the bad news is that sole proprietors have unlimited personal liability. This liability applies to business-related incidents—such as an accident on the premises—and debts arising from the business—such as purchase of supplies.

There may also be challenges to raising capital with the proprietorship choice. Because the business is wholly owned by the proprietor, there is no legal or structural mechanism to receive investment. Of course, assuming the proprietor can find a cooperative bank, loans to the proprietor are possible.

Your Turn

Please answer the following questions:

► Can you afford the risks involved in a sole proprietorship?

► Can you raise the capital necessary to begin?

► Have you spoken to any lending institutions about a loan?

EMPLOYEE ISSUES

Regardless of the legal form or structure of the business, an employer has certain minimal obligations to anyone who works for him or her. Therefore, sole proprietors must be prepared to obtain workers' compensation insurance and to contribute to state-sponsored programs like unemployment insurance. Likewise, the sole proprietor has to comply with all the requirements of the law that apply to any employer.

Chapter 8, Employment Law, Human Resources and Workplace Safety, discusses the legal obligation of employers to employees and workers to workers in greater detail.

TAX IMPLICATIONS

Tax treatment is sometimes considered an additional benefit of sole proprietorships. Since there is no legal or tax law distinction between a proprietorship and the individual owner, the sole proprietor reports income as part of the regular Form 1040 tax return and uses Schedule C to report business revenues and losses. This means that revenues from the business are included in ordinary income; expenses—losses—from the business are deductible to the extent permitted by the law.

The former vice president of a major national bank, a sophisticated investor who owns many rental properties and a major convenience store franchise, operates as a sole proprietor. He believes that this form gives him the best tax advantage, in spite of the potential personal liability from serving the general public in both his apartments and store; he considers these risks insurable. To him, having the ability to total all his revenues, deduct his operating expenses and apply his losses or gains to other income is an attractive benefit of the sole proprietorship form of organization.

If tax considerations factor into your choice of the business form, the sole proprietorship may be right for you. Before making this choice for tax purposes alone, check with your tax advisor.

CASE STUDY

Update on Laura's Business

In the beginning, the sole proprietor form was perfect for Laura. After all, it was her own business. And, things went well for The Laura Little Studio in its initial structure. Then, a large new car dealer asked Laura to design his logo, prepare his corporate image and handle his advertising. Laura was torn: on the one hand, this represented her first potentially profitable account; on the other hand, she knew she needed help to do the work. Her choices were to take on this big job and grow, or pass on the job and stay independent.

Laura accepted the assignment. She contacted Mary, a former colleague, and asked if Mary could moonlight. Mary could not do that; she reiterated her desire to work with Laura and suggested they work together. Laura offered Mary an hourly rate for her work or a salary; Mary refused, stating that she would not leave her current job unless she would be part of the new business.

Laura asked Mary to become a partner and Mary readily accepted Laura's offer. It became clear that Laura's business was outgrowing its sole proprietorship form.

Laura's situation is not unique. Many sole proprietors find that their business's potential and goals surpass the sole proprietorship form.

ASK YOURSELF

► Identify the pros and cons of the sole proprietorship as they relate to your business.

► Think about the tax implications of the sole proprietorship to your business.

► Evaluate how well your business fits the sole proprietor form.

► Consider whether you would be willing to expand to a partnership if you found yourself in a situation similar to Laura's.

CHAPTER
THREE

PARTNERSHIPS

TWO OR MORE?

Similar to the sole proprietorship, the partnership arises either automatically or by agreement. It provides for personal legal liability and tax responsibility to the partners and is simple to form and govern.

Partnerships usually arise automatically when two or more people engage in an organized activity without specifying another structure to govern their association. The law presumes that a partnership is intended when more than one principal operates a business without a written agreement.

A simple form of partnership agreement can be found in Appendix I as Exhibit 2.

HOW ARE PARTNERSHIPS FORMED?

To create a partnership, two or more people simply engage in the business. If there is considerable public contact or the partners want to protect and preserve a trade name, they should file a certificate of business.

The partnership form contains an important caveat:

> *If there is no written partnership agreement, the law implies certain minimum understandings between the parties, such as equal shares in profits and losses, plus the potential for full responsibility for debts.*

Since the law may impose an understanding different from that contemplated by the principals, it is strongly suggested that a written agreement be created if you select the partnership form.

Partnership agreements govern both the positive—for example, share of profits, measure of control—and negative—for example, percentage of liability for debts, restrictions of transferability—aspects of the working arrangement.

Take great care if you draft such a document. As with most legal arrangements carrying potential exposure, it is probably best to consult counsel. Alternatively, printed forms of partnership are sold in most larger stationery and bookstores.

Whether or not counsel is consulted, the following checklist should help assure that the agreement is complete.

Partnership Agreement Checklist

► What name will be used?

► How much capital contribution will each partner make and what percentage ownership will each have?

► What are the functional responsibilities of each partner? How much control will each have if shares are less than equal?

► If salaries—often referred to as draws in partnerships—are to be taken, how much will each get and when?

► Are bonuses to be granted? If so, by whom and when?

► How are profits and losses to be treated among the partners?

► What restrictions, if any, are there on other activities of partners—for example, prohibition against competing with the partnership?

► What will the duration of the partnership be? What guidelines are provided as to how the partnership is to be terminated?

► What provisions have been made for distribution of partnership assets—including goodwill, if any—upon dissolution? This clause should include a final accounting—maybe even an independent audit.

► Does the partnership agreement include a clause regarding dispute resolution? Mediation is suggested because of the nature of the relationship.

Your Turn   *Please answer the following questions:*

► Have you taken into consideration all of the items on the checklist?

► Does the balance of sharing profits and debts in a partnership appeal to you?

Good News/Bad News

Partnerships are ideal for close, trusting, working relationships. They allow partners a wide range of power and control. They are also the perfect vehicle for joint and equal financial contribution and a share in a venture.

As with sole proprietorships, the best news with partnerships is how easily they are formed. Partnerships have potential tax benefits called flow-through, whereby partners can deduct partnership losses and expenses against ordinary income. There is no double taxation, which is also true for corporations.

The bad news also relates to how easily they are formed. Sometimes a partnership can come into existence when it was not intended or when one party binds another to an obligation or debt, because the law implied a partnership out of the working relationship.

Also on the bad news side are:

▶ Difficulty in attracting nonpartner capital

▶ Lack of mechanism, such as shares of stock, to pass openly and freely

▶ Automatic termination provisions of the partnership law that include dissolution upon the death and, in some states, disability of a partner—a properly drawn agreement can get around automatic dissolution.

EMPLOYEE ISSUES

As with sole proprietorship, partners—as employers—are under legal obligation to employees.

With partnerships, it is important to make a distinction between a partner and an employee. Each may have intended that the worker be an employee; due to a lack of clarity about their working arrangement, the employee may be treated as a partner. This could mean that the worker could inadvertently waive his or her right to wages and could even be held responsible for a share of the debts. On the other hand, if the worker is held to be a partner, the worker could be entitled to a share of the profits.

Both of these contingencies can be adequately provided for in the partnership agreement and by a clear understanding between the employer—the partnership—and the employee that the employment arrangement is not a partnership agreement.

TAX IMPLICATIONS

Partnerships can have very attractive tax benefits. These benefits arise because, like a proprietorship, a partnership has no identity apart from its participants. The partnership is taxed through its participants; partners pay taxes at their own individual rates. While the partners may deduct their share of partnership losses, they must declare their share of partnership profits.

While not a legal entity for tax law or other liability purposes, the partnership must file a Partnership Tax Return (IRS Form 1065). This form is used for information purposes and not as the vehicle by which the taxes are collected.

Payments to the IRS—or deductions from losses—are indicated by the partnership distributing Schedule K-1 to its partners. Schedule K-1 is used as the worksheet for the partners when they fill out their individual Schedule E (Supplemental Income Schedule) forms and their Form 1040 returns; since the actual tax due calculations are made at the individual partners' tax rates, partners could end up paying different amounts in taxes.

On the surface, the flow-through aspects of tax treatment of partnerships appears an attractive feature. It usually is. However, remember that each partner's tax liability is calculated on the profitability of the partnership whether or not it distributes cash. Even when the partnership has a good year, the partnership may not want to distribute cash; yet, the partners could be liable to pay as if it did.

There are a number of other nuances to the tax laws that affect tax rates and deductibility of items for partners. These include such important factors as:

- ► Social Security, which cannot be deducted, since partner draws are not wages
- ► Certain employee fringe benefits, such as health and other insurance
- ► Some other benefit plans, which may not be deductible to the partners

Be aware:

- ► For tax purposes, the IRS will presume that any business with several persons participating in it for profit and/or loss is a partnership.

If your intent is to operate as a partnership, this is fine. However, if you are involved in a joint activity that is not a partnership or a corporation, get some good tax advice.

The caveat to get good tax advice should probably be a standard admonition to all partners, with the exception perhaps of those involved in the simplest of partnership undertakings.

LIMITED PARTNERSHIPS

Limited partnerships have the same attributes as general partnerships, and an additional unique feature that allows them to attract investors.

Briefly stated, a limited partnership has one or more general partners and one or more limited partners. The general partners have the same liabilities, responsibilities and control as in a regular partnership; the limited partners are liable only to the extent of their financial commitments to the firm. As long as they stay away from the day-to-day business of the firm, they are not liable for the general debts and obligations they would have if they were full, general partners. The law is very strict about this; in some states, limited partnerships are even required to be registered—somewhat like corporations.

Obvious benefits can be seen in this form where the general partners understand the business and the limited partners can provide financial support, but are not knowledgeable enough or are unwilling to run the risks of the liability of general partners.

Limited partnerships used to provide tax benefits beyond the amount of invested capital and were very attractive tax shelters. However, since tax reform, limited partners can only deduct as losses their legitimate share of the loss, bearing in mind the level of their risk. As with any other partnership agreement, while the limited partnership can allocate profit or loss as it sees fit, the IRS now looks closely at limited partners to assure that their deductions are appropriate for each limited partner's level of financial exposure or commitment in an endeavor.

Limited partnerships are still used to finance major projects such as:

▶ Real estate developments

▶ Energy production or exploration

▶ Motion pictures

The level of sophistication and need for carefully prepared legal documentation usually takes limited partnerships out of the mainstream of small business organization.

CASE STUDY

Update on Laura's Business

After a year of operations, The Laura Little Studio did really well. Mary became a 40% partner and earned a nice income on her share of the profits from that first year. Laura supplemented her income with draws from the firm; she took only 40% of the profit in cash, which left cash in the firm for continuing operations.

The ad campaign prepared by Laura and Mary for the car dealership was so successful that the regional distributor for the auto manufacturer requested that Laura bid on his entire New England region advertising business.

Laura and Mary knew that they could not handle an account of this magnitude without adding creative staff, beefing up their equipment and bringing in a full-time administrator/business manager. Assuming they got the job, Laura estimated that they would need to invest at least $100,000 of additional capital into the business to manage the regional auto account. In fact, Laura, Mary and Larry—who served as an unpaid advisor to the business—estimated that they would have to spend several thousand dollars just to prepare the proposal to the distributor.

They found themselves in a quandary. The business was doing quite well as it was. Mary and Laura got along well themselves and with their part-time copy writer and bookkeeper. They knew they would have to rent studio and office space and that they would run into a lot of hassles if they expanded. However, as Larry pointed out, the potential profit from this new job was too great to pass up. Besides, he contended, they might even be able to project enough profit to attract an outside investor to finance the expansion.

After a great deal of deliberation, Mary and Laura agreed to go after the job. They contacted the bank for the money to prepare the proposal. While the bank wished the women well, it turned down the loan, since the earlier loan to Laura and Larry was still unpaid—even though Laura had made all her interest payments in a timely fashion.

Laura called her dad. He was not able to help, since he had recently invested heavily in another project; instead, he suggested Ted, a friend of his who her dad thought might back the project for a share in the company without participation in the operation.

Laura, Mary and Ted met at Larry's attorney's office. In exchange for a 10% stake in their business, Ted offered the women $10,000 in seed capital to fund the preparation of the proposal.

After they discussed the options for Ted's participation, Laura asked Ted if he wanted to become a limited partner in The Laura Little Studio. Ted said that while he did not want to run the business or even to be part of everyday operations, "he never invested in a business in which he did not have a say."

Ted turned down the partnership because he did not want to be liable for any of the firm's debts. As an alternative, Ted asked if he could join Laura and Mary on their board of directors. It appeared as if it was now time to incorporate The Laura Little Studio.

ASK YOURSELF

► Compare the advantages and disadvantages to your business in forming a partnership.

► Discuss the merits of a limited partnership as an option for your business.

► What problems would the lack of stock options pose for your business?

CHAPTER FOUR

CORPORATIONS

WHAT IS A CORPO-RATION?

The principal difference between corporations and both sole proprietorships and partnerships is that corporations have a legal status of their own, independent of the people who work there, manage it or own it. This form of organization apparently grew out of the need for an entity with life longer than a "natural" person and with the ability to transact business on its own.[2]

Today, the existence of a corporation as a legal "person" is an accepted legal fiction, meaning that the law has decided to give the corporation certain human attributes. This legal fiction is well rooted in both statutory—written laws—and common law—case or decisional law.

Corporate law involves statutory considerations, which have resulted in a far more complex set of legal issues than for either sole proprietorships or partnerships. Since the corporation is a legal entity separate and apart from its human owners or operators, it has certain legal capabilities and obligations. Among these are:

- ► The ability to acquire, own or transfer property
- ► The ability to engage in contractual undertakings in its own right
- ► The power to hire and fire employees

Ownership in the corporation is evidenced by equity participation—that is, through shares. According to state law, these can be acquired in any fashion, including for cash, property or services rendered. Shareholders in a corporation own the firm. The shareholders have the right to elect directors; directors appoint or elect officers who are responsible for running the company. It has been said that directors are responsible for the strategic or long-term decisions, while officers are responsible for the tactical or short-term needs of managing the firm.

---

2. Hornstein. *Corporate Law and Practice,* St. Paul: West Publishing Co., 1959, pp. 10–12.

HOW ARE CORPORATIONS FORMED?

Unlike sole proprietorships and partnerships, corporations exist only by operation of law. Their lives depend completely upon statute. Each state has its own laws governing the formation, life, powers of and dissolution of corporate existence. Thus, to form a corporation, the parties—called promoters—who intend to form it must contact the official agency that handles corporate formation in the state and file the required forms. In most states, corporate formation is handled by the Secretary of State or a distinct state Division of Corporations.

While most states will accept formation documents—called Articles of Incorporation or Certificates of Incorporation—that contain a minimum amount of information, as illustrated in Exhibits 3A and 3B in Appendix I, they prefer that applicants use the state's own recommended—usually preprinted—format.

Most states also require that applicants use a specialized suffix for the business name, which shows the legal nature of the organization. Common suffixes include:

▶ Incorporated

▶ Corporation

▶ Inc.

In addition to the Articles of Incorporation, states require that a person or firm—usually residing in that state—be identified as an agent for service of process. This person or firm agrees that if the corporation is sued or if the state makes an official communication to the corporation, the state completes its legal obligation to serve the corporation when the statutory agent is served.

Each state charges a filing or registration fee and a tax on the shares is either issued or authorized. This franchise tax may be calculated on the number of shares that the corporation wishes to authorize—that is, to issue.

In addition to formation fees and forms, the state agency having jurisdiction will require annual reports from for-profit corporations and an annual fee for the corporation to remain in existence. Since the corporation exists only with the permission of the state, if fees are not paid or if a corporation acts beyond its powers, the state can revoke its corporate charter.

As discussed previously, one of the principal attributes of a corporation is its ability to continue to exist beyond the life of its incorporators—those who undertake the legal process of incorporation. The Articles of Incorporation specify how long the corporation will exist. The time period can even be specified as perpetual; this means that the corporation will continue to exist until it is dissolved by operation of law or by an act of dissolution by its principals.

Your Turn

Please answer the following questions:

> ► List the legal capabilities and obligations of a corporation.

> ► What is the role of the director of a corporation?

> ► What is the role of an officer in a corporation?

> ► What power does the state have over a corporation?

Good News/Bad News

The good news about corporations is the advantage they have over any other business form in the corporation's ability to continue to exist on its own. This allows the business to develop the potential for special value. Since ownership of a corporation is evidenced by shares and—unless there is an agreement prohibiting such transfers—the shares can be transferred, a corporation can raise money through sale of shares. Shares can also become valuable assets in the estate planning of stock owners.

Perhaps the best news about a corporation is the insulation of individuals from personal liability. Under both proprietorship and partnership, principals are personally liable for the debts, obligations and torts of their businesses. This is not true of corporations; since the corporation is a legal person for purposes of doing business, the corporation is liable for its own debts. Shareholder obligations are limited to the amount of money the shareholders agreed to invest or lend to the company.

While this sounds like a good way out of personal obligation, newer corporations or those with few assets will not usually qualify on their own for loans or other credit; their principals may need to sign personal guarantees.

A corporation has been called "cheap insurance against personal liability." In fact, most businesses in which the following is true should seriously consider the corporate form.

► Businesses that have constant and continuing public contact

► Businesses that sell a product

► Businesses that provide a service in which there is a potential for legal liability to third persons

If a corporation is not used, a principal could be sued after a mishap.

Make sure you are aware of the concept of piercing the corporate veil. This legal theory, which refers to the inability of a person to hide behind the corporate facade, is rarely used; however, the law might prevent insulation of liability if an individual creates confusion about what is a corporate or a personal obligation, or if an individual mixes corporate and personal assets. This concept can also apply where a parent company operates through a subsidiary merely to obscure liability.

Another important item to consider about the corporate form and liability is that while most of the so-called professions can now operate under a corporate umbrella—known in most states as PC for professional corporations or PA for professional associations—the corporate form cannot be used to insulate a person from the special fiduciary liability he or she has to their constituency. Therefore, a group medical practice that is incorporated cannot shield a physician from malpractice. And, where they are negligent, lawyers, architects and certain other "professions" which may now legally incorporate cannot hide behind a corporation.

The bad news is that corporations can be taxed doubly. Since a regular corporation is a person for tax purposes, the corporation may owe its own taxes in addition to the taxes individual shareholders pay on the wages and dividends they receive.

Another disadvantage of corporations is the necessity to comply with regulatory requirements, both in forming and in continuing to do business as a corporation. Companies that decide to sell their shares to the general public—if shares in the corporation are to be offered interstate—must register their offerings of shares at the federal level. The Securities and Exchange Commission (SEC) governs such offers. Registration requirements for the SEC are stringent to protect the public from fraudulent share offers.

Every state has its own securities registration requirements for intrastate offers. Known as Blue Sky Laws, these vary from a simple informational filing to elaborate advance clearance, similar to the SEC's requirements, by the state agency.

No company should even consider going public without the advice of qualified securities counsel and a financial advisor.

EMPLOYEE ISSUES

In corporations, the company is the employer. As such, the company has to comply with the legal requirements of appropriate personal and financial treatment of employees.

Most states also require strict compliance with working conditions and other related laws; states will snag individual officers or directors who violate these requirements.

The state has the ultimate power to close down the business. Even then, corporate officers who intentionally violate labor laws—including refusal or failure to pay wages—may be held personally liable. Check with your own state's labor department if you have concerns about this issue.

TAX IMPLICATIONS

For tax purposes, corporations are generally divided into two types.

- ▶ C-corporations, usually known as general business corporations
- ▶ S-corporations, usually known as small business corporations

There is little relationship between the size of the business and which of the corporate forms the principals select. Rather, the number of shareholders and how they want to file taxes dictates the appropriate form.

Generally speaking, a company that anticipates operational growth and the need for more than one principal stockholder or family member elects to be treated as a C-corporation. If so, both the corporation and shareholders are taxed. Any losses are reserved by the C-corporation against future earnings; they are not passed through to shareholders.

The corporate tax rate should be checked for both federal and state corporate taxes. Some states do not automatically tax corporate revenues, but have an optional franchise or "doing business" tax.

Successful companies should be aware of special provisions of the federal corporation tax laws that govern how much capital businesses can accumulate after business operating expenses, including wages and taxes, are paid. Usually, a portion of what remains—after a reserve for anticipated upcoming financial needs—is passed along to shareholders as dividends; these dividends are taxable to the shareholders on their own returns.

Since these dividends may not be deductible to the corporation and are taxable to the recipient, double taxation is obvious. Where the shareholder is also an operating employee, one answer to this problem is to pay the employee a larger salary, which is then taxed as part of the employee's personal tax obligation, and is deductible by the corporation as an operating expense. In this way, the additional income is additional wages, not subject to double taxation.

In some cases, a corporation can be used to provide fringe benefits and individual perks. While rules on deductibility of expenses have been tightened recently, corporate use of cars, business entertaining and travel, and expenses for some job-related educational courses should still be obtainable relatively tax-free. Retirement, medical and hospitalization, profit sharing and other financial security benefits may also have attractive tax consequences for shareholders.

Consult your tax professional for details on the perks the corporation may pay for and deduct as corporate expenses, and which benefits may be taxable to you as income.

An S-corporation may be the answer for businesses with primarily one or only a few shareholders—closely held. S-corporations are called corporations; but they are treated like individuals for tax purposes. S-corporations have similar tax flow-though provisions as partnerships and proprietorships. Shareholders of S-corporations have the benefit of shelter from liability, but they are not subject to the double taxation possibilities of C-corporations.

Since S-corporations have special tax treatment, there are some strict rules about taking this type of tax treatment election.

S-corporations are formed legally the same way any other corporation is formed. Soon after the business begins to function, the owners request S-corporation tax treatment by filing IRS Form 2553 with the IRS office for the area in which the corporation is located. The IRS will inform the applicants as to whether or not they meet the S-corporation guidelines.

S-corporation guidelines are, in essence, restrictions on corporate structure.

► The corporation must be a U.S.—domestic—corporation.

► The corporation may only have one class of stock.

► There can be no more than 35 shareholders.

► Shareholders must be natural persons—not corporations or partnerships.

► Every shareholder must be either a U.S. citizen or must legally reside in the U.S.

► The following corporations do not qualify as S-corporations:

  • Domestic international service corporations

  • Banks

  • Insurance companies

  • Companies receiving special Puerto Rico tax credit

  • Members of what the IRS calls affiliated groups

While S-corporations do not pay corporate income taxes, like partnerships they are required to file information returns. The S-corporation furnishes shareholders with information that the shareholders then report on their individual tax returns.

Important caveats about S-corporations:

► Some states do not share the federal government's view about S-corporation treatment. These states tax S-corporations like any other corporation.

► Since S-corporations are like privileged entities under the federal corporation tax laws, rules about their treatment are tightly enforced. Even though S-corporation treatment may be initially approved by the IRS, that status can be lost if the corporation engages in what the IRS believes is activity inconsistent with S-corporation guidelines.

Because of the complexities of corporate tax laws relating to both C- and S-corporations, consultation with your tax professional is strongly recommended.

Your Turn

Contact your neighborhood IRS office and request copies of tax forms and information sheets on partnerships, C-corporations and S-corporations:

► Compare the reporting and payment requirements.

► Speak with someone who operates a business or practice in each corporate form. Ask about their views of the tax issues and considerations.

NONPROFIT CORPORATIONS

Presumably, your business exists with a profit motive at its core. Sometimes, however, nonprofit corporations can serve a very valuable educational or auxiliary purpose to a profit-oriented business.

Like profit corporations, nonprofit—or not for profit—corporations exist as creatures of the state in which they are incorporated. Therefore, specific state forms and requirements for formation must be met.

► Nonprofit corporations do not have shareholders, although they can have members.

► No income, profit or distribution, other than legitimate wages or expenses, can be made to anyone in this type of structure.

► Unless it has been granted federal and/or state tax exemption, a nonprofit, like a profit corporation, must file periodic information returns and taxes.

Abuses and the need for additional government revenue has made nonprofit formation somewhat more challenging and requesting tax-exempt status far more challenging.

Creating a nonprofit can probably be done quite adequately on your own, but filing for tax exemption is virtually impossible without professional help.

CASE STUDY

Update on Laura's Business

After spending almost $8,000 on their proposal, The Laura Little Group, Inc. (the "Group," as the incorporated business became known) did not get the regional distributorship advertising business. However, they did land two additional individual car dealers as clients and, as a result, had to move into new studio and office space.

After several years, the Group was billing more than $1 million; they had about a dozen employees as well as freelance people. Ted made a positive contribution to long-term planning during biweekly board of directors meetings; Laura was pleased that Ted was on the board and available for advice.

One day, Ted called Laura very excitedly. He had met a young artist, Penny. Penny had developed a cartoon character for ecology marketing, called Greenie. Ted felt Greenie might be a valuable property and an excellent item for licensing for use to others.

Penny needed to prepare a portfolio and presentation so she could market her concept to industry; she had called Ted to invest in Greenie. Ted mentioned to Penny that he was a shareholder in an advertising and design firm and that he would try to get the firm to invest time and materials into developing Greenie for sale.

Laura, Mary and Ted met over lunch, then held a special board of directors meeting to discuss the project. They decided that the Group was willing to undertake some design and other work, including creation of a formal presentation that included copy.

When Ted contacted Penny to ask if she would license the whole Greenie concept to the Group, Penny mentioned that she had her own family corporation and wanted to keep the property there; she suggested that the Group could become shareholders in her company.

As much as Laura, Mary and Ted wanted equity in the project for the Group, they did not want to be directly in business with Penny. Again, they called on Larry's attorney, who now also represented the Group. He suggested a joint venture.

ASK YOURSELF

▶ Compare the pros and cons of incorporating your business.

▶ How would the legal status of the corporation be beneficial or detrimental to your business?

▶ Explain the potential effects of franchise tax and potential double taxation on your business.

▶ What are the labor laws in your state? What are the penalties for violation?

▶ Discuss the appropriateness of C-corporation and S-corporation status for your business.

CHAPTER
FIVE

JOINT
VENTURES

WHAT IS A JOINT VENTURE?

A joint venture is an undertaking by two or more persons or organizations to share the expense and profit of a particular project. This strategy can be used when something needs to be done that needs resources or input beyond your capability, and which does not require a formal business organization be formed to undertake it.

HOW IS A JOINT VENTURE FORMED?

Joint ventures are not business organizations in the sense of proprietorships, partnerships or corporations. They are agreements between parties or firms for a particular purpose or venture. Their formation may be very informal, such as a handshake and an agreement for two firms to share a booth at a trade show. Other arrangements can be extremely complex, such as the consortium of major U.S. electronics firms to develop new microchips.

Joint ventures are governed by the agreement that brings them into being. Unless the joint venture is formalized by creation of a corporation or partnership, it never ripens into a tax-paying, legal entity on its own. Instead, the joint venture functions through the legal status of the venture participants, known as co-venturers or venture partners. A joint venture is, in effect, a form of partnership that is limited to a particular purpose. Many times, joint ventures take on formalized partnership forms. A sample joint venture agreement can be found in Appendix I as Exhibit 4.

Since the joint venture is not a legal entity on its own, it does not hire people, enter into contracts or have its own tax liabilities. These matters are handled through the co-venturers.

Corporate law, partnership law and the law of sole proprietorship do not govern joint ventures; contract law governs joint ventures.

ASK YOURSELF

► After considering the legal ramifications and implications, how do you feel about doing business on your own?

► Discuss the reasons why one form of business organization seems best suited to your personal, business and long-term needs.

► Discuss your preparation for fulfilling the legal requirements and other regulatory and procedural requirements of owning your own business.

CHAPTER
SIX

CONTRACTS

THE BASICS

An oral contract is not worth the paper it's written on.

—Leo Rosten

There is a temptation to get very legalistic when talking about contracts. In truth, a contract is simply an undertaking or promise between two or more people or entities to do something or to refrain from doing something for which value has been given from promisor to promisee.

In most cases, it makes no difference whether or not there is a written agreement.

The terms *contract* and *agreement* are synonymous for purposes of this discussion. In business, when you hear someone refer to an agreement, it is safe to presume they mean *contract*. Because of the possibility of misunderstanding between a contract and an agreement—which is not necessarily legally binding—the term *contract* is used in this chapter.

Whether we are aware of it or not, contracts between parties and organizations are the way we do things. Virtually every commercial transaction, and many personal transactions, involves a contract of some type.

- ► When we shop in a store, we contract to purchase.

- ► When we eat at a restaurant, we contract for services and food.

- ► When we write a check, we contract to pay.

- ► When we hire someone to paint the house, we contract for services.

HOW CONTRACTS COME ABOUT

Legal obligations in contract can arise in two ways.

1. Through an *express contract*, where a party expresses a specific intention to be bound by contract

2. Through an *implied contract*, where the conduct of the party is such that it is assumed that he or she means to enter into a contract

Obviously, expressly written contracts are less likely to lead to confusion or disputes. The express contract represents your intentions about the transaction in your own words. On the other hand, if your conduct would lead one to believe that you intended there to be a contract, the law will imply one, rather than do injustice to the other side.

For example:

Express contract: I agree with the painter to paint my house and sign the proposal.

Implied contract: I drive my car to the car wash and get in the wash line.

Another way to classify contracts is by the timing in which the action that is required under the contract—the performance—is due. Contracts that call for some kind of immediate action are referred to as *executed* or *present* contracts; contracts that envision performance at some time in the future are considered *executory*.

For example:

Present or executed contract: I make an appointment to have the plumbing in my house fixed. When the plumber comes and does the work, I must pay.

Executory contract: I enter into an agreement to purchase a pedigree pup as soon as it can leave its mother. When the pup is ready and I pay any balance due, I can bring the puppy home.

Every contract has certain minimum basic requirements to be binding on the parties.

Contract Basics Include

▶ **An offer**, which is a proposal that leads to a contract when accepted. It can also be thought of as an invitation to engage in the planned undertaking, although, technically speaking, an invitation is not an offer.

▶ **Acceptance**, which is the acknowledgment by the offeree to proceed into the contractual relationship.

▶ **Consideration**, which is the value exchanged by the parties to pay for the undertaking. Consideration is usually money, but also can be in goods or services or anything of value.

▶ **Legal purpose**, which gives the contract meaning. Contracts that are for illegal purposes are void from the beginning and give no one any legal rights.

▶ **Capacity**, which is the legal power to enter into and understand the nature of the contracting process. This usually applies to being of legal age or of appropriate mental capacity to understand what a contract is.

Once all the basics are in place, the contract comes about.

CASE STUDY

Laura Little's Remodel

Laura has decided to have part of the studio remodeled. She requests bids from several construction firms. As each builder sends in a bid, Laura receives an offer—that is, the builder offers to do the work for the quoted sum.

The best bid is from the Bill Ditt Company. For $16,000, the company will remodel two large studio rooms, including building in shelves and ceiling lighting.

Bill stops by The Laura Little Studio. Laura signs a written form indicating her acceptance; she gives Bill a deposit so that he can purchase supplies. Laura and Bill agree that Bill will get any official license or permission necessary to do the job and that he will complete the job within three weeks.

The elements in Laura's situation are:

The offer: Bill will remodel the studio for $16,000.

The acceptance: Laura agrees to the proposal in writing.

Consideration: Laura promises to pay money in exchange for labor and materials.

Legal purpose: This assumes the building was properly zoned and necessary permits were obtained.

Capacity: Laura is an adult, capable of understanding the nature of the transaction and entering into the contract.

The contract between Bill and Laura is completed, giving each party certain rights and obligations.

In this case, there was a written agreement, but not all contracts need be in writing. In fact, most of our daily agreements arise out of oral communications.

WHAT AGREEMENTS SHOULD BE IN WRITING?

To prevent fraud, certain types of agreements are required by law to be in writing. These include:

▶ Contracts involving nearly all real estate transactions

▶ Contracts for the sale of goods of a value over a certain sum—often $500

▶ Contracts that cannot be fully performed within one year

The law governing which agreements must be in writing is called the *Statute of Frauds*. In each state, the Statute of Frauds specifies the particular agreements that have to be in writing to be enforceable. In many states, the Statute of

Frauds is included in the Uniform Commercial Code (UCC). Chapter 7, Commercial Instruments, includes a discussion of the UCC.

In Laura's contract with Bill for remodeling, time of completion was mentioned specifically. This means that if Bill does not complete the job in time, Laura has a remedy against him for breach of contract. If time had not been mentioned, the law would imply a *reasonable time* for the completion of the contract.

Your Turn   ***Please answer the following questions:***

> ► What are the two types of contracts?

> ► List the two ways legal obligations can arise within a contract.

> ► In your state, which contracts must be in writing?

WHAT CONTRACT TERMS THE LAW WILL IMPLY

If the parties to a contract have not provided their own terms in certain areas, the law will imply terms in the contract to fill in the gaps. Among the contract provisions a court will imply are:

► Reasonable time for performance.

► Assignability to anyone who succeeds to the interest of either party.

► The law governing the contract will be the law of the place—jurisdiction—where the contract came into being.

► All prior communications about the subject are incorporated into the contract. This means that no evidence can be introduced showing earlier negotiations.

► The party signing the contract was authorized to do so and intended his or her act.

► Without stating specific standards, a reasonable standard of performance of the contract was intended.

► Delivery and payment should take place simultaneously.

► There are no special conditions not named in the contract.

► Insolvency terminates the agreement.

► In the event of default, money damages will suffice.

Rather than relying on these implications by operation of law, the parties should spell out in detail, within the document, all significant terms. It is far better to err by saying more than you think is necessary in a contract than by leaving out an important provision.

In reality, we engage in our own contracts and agreements every day, and almost always without consulting counsel. However, when you are negotiating an important agreement that carries with it provisions obligating you to do something or pay for something, and that agreement goes beyond the routine activities of your business, it is probably best to have the document drafted—or at least reviewed—by counsel.

When this is not possible, use this checklist:

Checklist for Writing or Reviewing a Contract

► Is the subject matter of the contract described in detail— e.g., the property covered, the lot number, serial number?

► By law, does this agreement have to be in writing?

► Are the parties to be bound by the agreement clearly identified? Have they signed or otherwise agreed?

► Has the consideration been specified in sufficient detail?

► Are there any conditions that must be met before the contracts take effect?

► Are all prior communications about the subject merged into or superseded by the contract?

► Are you relying on the other party's specific representations? If so, do they appear in the written agreement?

► Do you have the necessary power and legal authority to enter into this agreement? What about the other side?

► What is the term—the length of time—of the contract?

► Is there any provision in the agreement that should survive the specified term?

► Are there any specific warranties—special undertakings or guarantees—that should be included?

► Is performance of the contract needed at a specific time? If so, have you added a clause saying: "Time is of the essence in this agreement"?

► Have you made provision for unlikely circumstances or acts of God—*force majeure*?

► Is there to be collateral security—that is, something outside the agreement—given as part of the transaction?

► Must there be any provision regarding property rights?

► Should there be a liquidated damages clause? If not mentioned, regular contract damages alone will apply.

► Have you provided for adequate notice, with a time to cure any default?

► Is the law of a particular state more advantageous than another? If so, have you provided for *controlling law*?

► Should the contract be assignable? If so, to whom and under what circumstances?

► What happens upon insolvency or legal declaration of bankruptcy?

► Who bears the risk of loss and the duty to insure at various points in the agreement?

- ▶ Is there a provision for modification of the agreement; if so, does it require written modification?

- ▶ If one or more provisions are unenforceable, is the whole contract unenforceable?

- ▶ Does your agreement need an escape clause? If so, will it run one way or both ways?

- ▶ Should the agreement bind the heirs or successors of either or both parties?

- ▶ Have you specified what constitutes default or a breach of the agreement?

- ▶ Have you specified dispute resolution or made other provision for what happens on default such as mediation and/or arbitration?

This checklist is not intended to substitute for advice on how to write a contract. However, you might want to use it in conjunction with the samples included as Exhibits 12–15 in Appendix I to give you a basic understanding of the variety of contracts and critical information they should contain.

Contracts arise out of the intentions of the parties, as expressed in writing or orally. Express contracts are better than implied contracts because the parties' own wishes are clear from the language. In impled contracts, the legal decision makers—a lawyer, judge or jury—will have to try to figure what was meant from the conduct of the parties.

WHAT IS A *QUASI-CONTRACT*?

Sometimes, the law will go so far as to create a contract-like relationship to prevent *unjust enrichment* by one side. This area, known as *quasi-contract*, was used by the courts of equity to protect one side from undue advantage by the other—especially where the event arose innocently or accidentally. The concept of quasi-contract can seem a bit obtuse, so let's see it in use by Bill Ditt.

CASE STUDY

Bill Ditt and His Construction Firm

Bill Ditt visited the Smith residence at the request of Mrs. Smith, who told Bill that Mr. Smith was away on a long business trip; she wanted to surprise him by adding a deck to the back of their house. Bill made an oral quote that Mrs. Smith accepted orally. Bill sent a crew out to do the work. When the job was completed, Bill handed Mrs. Smith a statement for his services, which Mrs. Smith told Bill she would have her husband pay when he returned.

When Mr. Smith returned, he was upset that the work was done; he refused to pay Bill's invoice. When Bill called him, Mr. Smith said that he owns the house and had never contracted for any work. He insisted that he is not going to pay.

Is Bill out of luck?

The answer is a partial *yes* and a partial *no*.

Bill cannot be paid the full contract amount if, in fact, Mrs. Smith did not have the authority to enter into a binding contract—although she may have been an *apparent agent*. That's the bad news.

The goods news is that under the concept of *quasi-contract*, the law will not let Mr. and Mrs. Smith benefit from this misunderstanding. So, if Mr. Smith kept the deck, he would have to pay the *reasonable value* of the work. This payment would be made pursuant to a legal theory imposed to prevent unjust enrichment. Such reasonable payment may be less than the full contract price, but Bill Ditt would not have lost everything.

The lesson here is to know when you are about to enter into contractual relationships and to try to control the terms by creating an express contract.

REMEDIES FOR BREACH OF CONTRACT

What happens if one party fails to perform as agreed?

Under noncontract theories of law, such as negligence or defamation, the measure of damages for a breach of duty or improper conduct is the sum that will make the party whole. Sometimes this includes indirect damages and even pain and suffering.

Where there is a contract and there has been a breach, the innocent party may bring a legal action against the breaching party. This is referred to as a *default*. The remedy is to seek recovery of money damages or try to get the contract performed.

Where money damages are sufficient to compensate the party wronged, they will be awarded.

Where money damages alone are inadequate to give fair recovery, the court may issue an *injunction* forcing one side to do something—that is, perform the contract. This situation is quite rare, since money can usually cure a defect in the contract process.

As the measure of damages for determining the amount of the award for breach of contract, the courts will refer to the sum necessary to make the party whole or put him/her in the position he or she would have been in had the contract been performed.

To illustrate, let's refer back to Laura Little's contract with Bill Ditt. Suppose that when Bill was half done with the work—and had been paid $8,000—he got the chance to do a bigger and more profitable job. Suppose Bill's crew did not show up to finish the job, so Laura would call Bill. Laura might be put off continuously until Bill would finally admit that he would not finish the work. Laura would then call her attorney who would advise her that she could have the work done elsewhere.

Let's suppose the cheapest bid she could get was $9,600. Under the law, Bill would be liable for $1,600 and Laura for $8,000. Thus, Laura would be in the same position she would have been in if the original contract had been performed.

Could Laura have forced Bill to finish the job as planned?
Only in extreme circumstances will a court take action to force someone to do something.

There are some tests:

► If Laura has an adequate remedy at law—that is, if money damages will suffice—there will be no injunctive relief.

► If Bill does not obey the court order, can the court get jurisdiction—legal power over the party in question—to force compliance with the contract terms by injunction with the power of contempt?

In this case, before a court would give her what the law calls *specific performance*—a mandatory injunction—Laura would have to show the court that she could get certain work only from Bill or that there was no other resource for getting that work done.

Since it is highly unlikely that a court will force someone to specifically perform a contract, the safest approach is to assure yourself that you can be made whole through money damages, by getting someone else to perform a breached agreement.

If the particular transaction requires some type of unique or special performance—such as painting a portrait or purchase of something with value, besides money—be certain that the contract includes a clause acknowledging that you do not have an adequate remedy at law and requiring the other side to submit to injunctive relief.

Even this kind of language does not guarantee that the court will award specific performance, but it does increase the chances.

On the other hand, if you are the party who is to perform under a contract, use every effort to avoid agreeing to such language. Certainly, some contractual undertakings may require unique performance, but try to limit your own liability to money damages in the event of default. Also, try to obtain a curing clause that may allow you some time to deal with the alleged breach.

A number of contract forms—leases, bills of sale, promissory notes, etc.—are available from bookstores and stationery houses in standardized forms and printed versions. While these forms can meet many usual needs of many business and personal transactions, take great care not to inadvertently waive contract rights or to encumber a transaction with unnecessary verbiage. Watch for compliance with local laws and use only standard or printed forms in the state where you expect the contract to come into legal existence.

Your Turn

Please answer the following questions:

▶ Define *quasi-contract* and list its benefits.

• Definition: _____

• Benefits: _____

▶ What steps are taken when a breach of contract occurs?

▶ Define specific performance.

EMPLOYMENT AGREEMENTS

Employers and employees should be explicit about their proposed relationships. If an employment contract is intended, specify the terms. Most states acknowledge the right of the employer to terminate the employee at any time and the corollary right of the employee to quit at any time.

If the intention of the hiring person or firm is to create an employment-*at-will relationship* in which the employer reserves the right to terminate at any time for any reason, be alert to the following exceptions created by court decisions in most jurisdictions:

► An employee cannot be terminated for being asked to violate a law or violating another public policy requirement, such as whistle blowing.

► Where an implied contract for a specific term or other conditions is created at the hiring interview or later in the employment term, the employer may not be able to deny the contract easily.

► There is sometimes an *implied covenant of good faith and fair dealing*. This esoteric—and perhaps archaic—precept stands for the premise that an employee can only be terminated for *good cause*. While this exception to the *at will* concept of employment is not now widely held, be aware that an employee who thinks he or she has been unfairly terminated may very well allege it.

Agreements creating agency relationships, consultancies and other work-type arrangements are vulnerable to allegations of implied contract. From this vulnerability to court imposition of implied terms, the conclusion must be drawn that whenever you bring a person—or a firm—in to do a particular assignment or as a regular employee, you need to be clear about all terms in both written and oral representations about the proposed work and the length of the proposed employment.

In Appendix I you will find examples of an employment agreement (Exhibit 5) and independent consulting contract (Exhibit 6).

ASK YOURSELF

▶ To assess the effect of contracts in your work or everyday life, make a list or keep a journal of each transaction in your day that involves a contract or an agreement.

- Assess which of the agreements you are involved with that might need some legal advice or other expert thought before you enter into them. Identify the type of advice or thought required.

- Describe the contracts in your work that can be standardized.

CHAPTER
SEVEN

COMMERCIAL
INSTRUMENTS

THE UCC MODEL

Most commercial transactions in the United States are governed by the Uniform Commercial Code (UCC). Like other "Uniform Laws," the UCC was developed as a model code to simplify transactions that involve commerce between persons and organizations and from state to state.

The UCC covers a number of topic areas. The preamble speaks of:

▶ *Certain Commercial Transactions in or regarding Personal property and Contracts and other Documents concerning them, including Sales, Commercial Paper . . . Bills of Lading, other Documents of Title . . . Secured Transactions.*

The UCC applies to the kinds of transactions you can expect to participate in as you conduct everyday business. These include:

▶ Purchase and sales of individual goods—i.e., consumer transactions

▶ Bulk sales—special sales that are not "held in the ordinary course of business"

▶ Use of checks, notes and other negotiable instruments

While the UCC is a model code, it has been adopted in almost full form in nearly every state. Louisiana, one exception, has adopted only portions of the code. Check the codes in your area for the variations in your particular locale.

The references in this chapter are intended to help you research a point further in your local laws.

Your Turn

Contact an attorney or check your local law library for cross references to the Uniform Commercial Code to learn more about the commercial laws that apply to your business and are in force in your state.

WHAT TO EXPECT

Some generalizations apply to the kinds of matters you can expect to be involved in with the UCC as you do business.

Negotiable Instruments

The law has developed the concept of *negotiability* with respect to certain documents to allow for the free flow of commerce. This means that, on its face, the document has legal and monetary significance. A key element in negotiability is the acceptance of the document—referred to by lawyers as an *instrument*—by the recipient, in lieu of money or as evidence of money or other things of value. Checks and promissory notes are examples of negotiable instruments.

Other key attributes of negotiability in an instrument are the ease with which it can be transferred and the legal implications of the transfer and possession of the document. Instruments that are negotiable can be transferred to anyone willing to accept them, and they represent the values inscribed on their faces.

For example:

► You received a note for $5,000 from Joe in exchange for some equipment you sold him. You have the legal right to transfer the note to anyone who wants it.

► Later, Jim offers you $4,000 for the note. You need the cash; Joe's note is not due for 60 days and you cannot afford to wait. You transfer the note to Jim for the $4,000 cash. Joe now owes $5,000 to Jim, even if the equipment turns out to be defective.

In this context, the act of transfer is referred to as *negotiation*. The recipient of the instrument is known as the *holder*. If the transfer has been made in the ordinary course of business, the recipient is known as a *holder in due course*. This means that he or she has certain legal rights flowing from the receipt of the instrument. The UCC specifies what these rights will be.

Where the instrument is payable to the bearer, the negotiation—legal transfer—is complete by delivery of the instrument. Assuming he or she received the instrument properly, the bearer has all the legal rights in the document without further need for action. A bearer instrument is virtually the same as money. Your possession of it gives you all rights to use it freely.

If the instrument is not a bearer document—if instead, it is payable to a particular party (such as a check made "payable to the order of Sally Jones"), the instrument can be negotiated only through proper endorsement by Sally.

In the example of Jim and Joe, if Jim gives you a $4,000 check payable to you and you want to pay Jane money you owe her, you can endorse the check over to her. You can do so by writing in the endorsement portion on the back of the check:

> *Pay to the order of Jane. . . .*

You would then sign—endorse—the check with your own name.

This is known as a *special endorsement*: it specifies the person to whom the instrument has been endorsed. If you merely signed your name, the endorsement would be considered an *endorsement in blank*.

The danger in using endorsements in blank is that once the instrument has been endorsed, it becomes a bearer instrument: anyone who possesses it can have the financial benefit of it. Clearly, such endorsements can invite theft.

The *restrictive endorsement* is another type of endorsement on a negotiable instrument. Phrases such as *For deposit only* and *pay the XYZ bank* restrict the use of the instrument; the restrictive endorsement is much safer when using checks.

Checks that are accumulated for some time before deposit or are transported should bear a special or restrictive endorsement.

Please answer the following questions:

▶ What are two examples of negotiable instruments?

Define:

• Negotiable

• Holder

• Holder in due course

• Special endorsements

• Restrictive endorsements

What Is the UCC Responsible For?

Article III of the UCC specifies the formalities required to make instruments negotiable under the code. Even though some local laws have modified the UCC, all states have adopted the negotiability standard. An instrument must meet certain minimum criteria to be negotiable in the United States.

Minimum Criteria for a Negotiable Instrument

▶ The instrument must be in writing and signed by the person on whose account the instrument is dependent—the maker—or upon whom it shall be paid—the drawer. There must be a clear and unconditional promise to pay a certain sum in money. The instrument must be payable at a time specified clearly in the instrument or on demand—that is, at any time at the wish of the holder.

▶ It must be made payable to a specific person or to bearer.

Each of these requirements is a mandatory minimum and cannot be waived. If any requirement is missing, the bank or maker can refuse to pay or honor it.

When you accept a note or other promise to pay from someone—including a check—make sure that all the components listed above are clear on the face of the document.

Exhibit 7 in Appendix I is a sample promissory note—which is also, of course, a contract to pay.

Checks

The following checklist will help you avoid disappointment, delay and money loss from accepting a check that proves not to be "good."

Checklist for Checks

▶ Is the check printed with the name and address of the drawer?

▶ Does the person issuing the check seem of sound mind—i.e., not under duress or under the influence of drugs or alcohol?

▶ Is the check drawn specifically to you or is it drawn to the order of someone else and endorsed over to you? *Accepting the latter carries high risk.*

▶ Does the check bear a printed number that indicates it is not a new account? *Avoid accepting checks with one or two digit numbers or with numbers in the 100 series.*

▶ Has the person issuing the check asked you to hold it? Has he or she postdated it? *In either situation, the chances of it not being "good" are far greater than a check issued for immediate deposit against good funds—i.e., money currently in the drawer's account.*

▶ Have you received a bad check or had a bad credit experience with this person before? *If so, proceed cautiously.*

▶ Have you checked the appropriate identification of the drawer—unless that person is known to you? *If possible, proper identification should include some type of official government picture identification. Be alert for stolen identification and be aware of how easy it is to make fake identification.*

▶ Have you made a note of back-up information—such as employer name and phone—on the face of the check, in case you need to collect on the check? *In case they have to make an identification later to establish that the person in question issued the check, some people even make a note of the sex, birth date, height, weight, hair and eye colors, and race of the person tendering the check. Noting these factors for identification purposes only does not violate civil rights or related laws.*

Criminal sanctions for issuing "bad checks" vary from state to state. In some jurisdictions, most check cases are considered civil wrongs and the state prosecutor will not be of much help. In other states, issuing a bad check can be a serious crime and threat of court action can yield dramatic collection results.

Be aware of this important caveat:

> *Before you accuse a person of a crime—such as issuing a bad check—make sure you understand the local treatment of such issues. If you are alleging a crime, make sure the check incident was not a genuine mistake or misunderstanding. You would not want to face a charge of malicious prosecution or defamation for making an unfounded allegation. Follow recommended procedures to try to collect—for example, send a notice by certified mail. If the recommended procedures fail, request a warrant.*

Sales

Since the UCC governs most commercial transactions in virtually all states, when you are engaged in the sale or purchase of goods—a contract—you can expect that the UCC will probably apply in some fashion. Article II of the UCC is based upon a prior law, known as the Uniform Sales Act, which is structured in terms of a sales contract and the terms needed for performance.

Under the prior law, delivery of property or title determined legal rights. Under the UCC's Article II, the written document itself has control. In fact, most contracts for the sale of goods—usually those valued at $500 or more—or contracts that cannot be fully performed within one year are required to be in writing. This rule arose from an old English law called the Statute of Frauds, designed to protect people from criminal business practices.

Today, the Statute of Frauds is part of the UCC. Written contracts cannot be varied by evidence of prior or contemporaneous conversation or negotiations—the presumption being that the document fully reflects the agreement of the parties.[3] According to the terms of the agreement, modifications of the understanding must be in writing.

When a contract refers to sales of goods, reference must also be made to the UCC with regard to what constitutes offer[4] or acceptance[5]. Rules regarding modifications of these types of contracts are covered in Section 2-207 of the UCC.

A *warranty* may be considered almost a separate contract within the main contract. Under warranty law, promises about the way products are or how they work are either express—actually stated—or implied by the law. Often, warranties are given with regard to sales.

The Magnuson-Moss Act is a federal law that requires specific warranty language for all sales of goods to consumers. This Act does not replace either UCC requirements as to warranties or state laws regarding consumer protection. If you are engaged in selling products to consumers, you must become familiar with Magnuson-Moss requirements.

According to the Magnuson-Moss Act, written warranties covering sales of products costing $15 or more must specify:

- ► Who the warranty covers
- ► The part or parts of the product that are covered
- ► What will be done by the warrantor—the person giving the warranty—including identification of what the warrantor will pay for and what the consumer must pay for
- ► The date the warranty is effective, if this date is different from the purchase date

---

3. See Section 2-201 of the UCC.
4. See Section 2-205 of the UCC.
5. See Section 2-206 of the UCC.

► How the consumer can obtain benefits under the warranty, including addresses and instructions as to what to send, when and where

Other provisions of the UCC covering sales include:

► **Sections 2-315 and 2-317:** Need for adequate description of goods

► **Section 2-305:** Price provisions

► **Section 2-208:** Delivery time and place

► **Section 2-401:** Passage of title

► **Sections 2-509 and 2-510:** Who shall bear the risk of loss

Several other sections cover specific conditions of delivery and shipment method.

In the event of a breach of the contract of sale, both the seller and the buyer have remedies. These include:

► The seller's rights to react to the buyer's insolvency

► Repudiation of the contract

► Failure to cooperate

► Other conduct inconsistent with the sale.[6]

If the seller breaches the agreement, the buyer's remedies include the right to reject the goods or cancel the performance and are also covered in the UCC.[7]

Entitlement to damages for such failures of sales agreements including the measure of damages are determined by the usual contract damages rules—that is, placing the party where he or she would have been, had the agreement been fulfilled.[8]

Exhibit 8 in Appendix I is a sample bill of sale.

---

6. See UCC Sections 2-701 through 2-710 for more details.

7. See UCC Sections 2-607 to 2-610 and 2-710 to 2-715 for more details.

8. The UCC specifies other remedies in Section 2-708.

List the federal provisions that cover sales:

► _____

► _____

► _____

► _____

We have been discussing general sales so far, but suppose the sale is to be according to a secured transaction—for example, title is in some way reserved pending payment—or is a bulk sale—for example, an entire inventory? The following legal considerations involve two important commercial transaction possibilities:

► Secured transactions

► Credit

Secured transactions are commercial transactions where one party retains some property rights in a thing of value to secure the full performance of the other's obligation. Conditional sales and loans secured by a lien on property are common secured transactions. Using this type of financial arrangement allows some safety in extending credit from the creditor—the lender—to the debtor—borrower.

If the credit arrangement is set up properly, the creditor's interest in the property pledged as security by the debtor is secure, even if the debtor tries to sell or transfer the property to someone else. In fact, the rationale behind these laws is to protect creditors from intentional or accidental loss of the security for the debt.

Secured means that one person or firm maintains a property right in some property or thing of value of another person or firm. *Mortgage* connotes a secured transaction, as does *lien* and *deed of trust*; these are basically the same thing. As with all secured transactions, certain procedures must be followed for liens to be binding on the party to be charged—the debtor—and to serve as *notice* to the rest of the world. In this context, the term *notice* means that all people involved with the property in question are presumed by the law to know about the security interest.

Permission of the debtor is usually required before a security interest can be *perfected*—put into place as required by law. Certain transactions can provide automatically for the institution of a lien.

For example, if a mechanic works on your car or a carpenter works on your house, he or she may have a lien for unpaid bills against the property. While these liens arise automatically and do not need the permission of the debtor, they require certain filing to serve as notice to all others.

Check your local laws if you are involved in a business where you may be able to get a lien by operation of law.

How are these security interests perfected?

Under Article 9 of the UCC, two basic steps are required to gain the legal priority of claims against the secured property:

1. The creditor takes physical possession of the property in question.

2. The creditor files a financing statement in the appropriate form at the appropriate place.

Check your local laws to see where and how financing statements are filed in your state. Some jurisdictions accomplish this at the local or county level, usually at the courthouse; in others, the state maintains a central filing location, sometimes in the office of the Secretary of State.

The principal purpose of the secured transaction is to protect the creditor. Therefore, the UCC is explicit in its requirements, which insure that the security interest is binding and complete and gives the creditor priority over other creditors—at least with respect to the item secured.

The following checklist should help you comply with the UCC conditions for secured transactions:

Secured Transaction Checklist

▶ Is the agreement in writing? Most secured transactions must be in writing.

▶ Is the collateral that is the subject matter of the secured transaction clearly identified?

▶ Other than those of the debtor, are there other claims or property interests in the collateral?

▶ In whose possession is the collateral?

▶ Does the debtor have liens or other obligations?

▶ Does a spouse or anyone else have claims on the property?

▶ In the future, will there be additions to the collateral?

▶ Which of the following Article 9 descriptions apply to the collateral?
  • Goods
  • Documents of title
  • Accounts or other intangibles
  • Items likely to become fixtures—that is, they are attached to real estate, such as a book case affixed permanently to the wall
  • Purchase money security interest—that is, secured debt owned by the debtor

▶ Does the security agreement contain sufficient language, as required by the UCC?

▶ Is there a valid and properly worded loan note underlying the security claim?

▶ Has the loan note complied with all provisions of law— for example, legal interest rate, truth in lending law?

Promptness in filing the claim of security interest is usually what counts, rather than possession or even earlier legal claim to the goods. As a result, races to the Secretary of State or courthouse to file notice of secured interest are common.

Securing a debt under the UCC is a reasonable way to make sure you will be paid. Be certain to adhere to the procedural guidelines for obtaining your priority of claim against the secured goods. The office of the agency that records the claims will have the guidelines and requirements—as will attorneys versed in commercial law and many accountants.

LIENS

Liens are governed by state laws, which are not nearly as uniform as the UCC. In addition to liens obtained by securing collateral under the UCC:

▶ Liens can be attached to property.

▶ Liens can arise out of common law—that is, decisions by courts, acknowledging the legality of such liens. These include liens for services—usually called *mechanic's liens*—and liens for supplies or materials—usually called *material liens*.

Under most state's laws, liens that arise by statute or common law, including recognized business practice, may have priority over all other liens—even those where an attempt is made to secure the loan.[9]

When it comes to credit and commercial transactions, the rights of a person who has no notice of someone else's alleged claim in goods is often in question. The UCC deals specifically with these issues under the theory of the *bona fide purchaser for value without notice*. Although situations vary as to who gets what, it is probably fair to say that the person who has completed a legal claim under the UCC has priority over a person who may have obtained goods in good conscience, but has not completed a legal claim.

This may sound tough, but the law has determined that this is the way people can take legal comfort in commercial transactions. As to the UCC, if you have complied with it,

---

9. See UCC Section 9-310 for important information about the priority of liens.

shouldn't you be able to assert your legal rights against anyone else?

If you are involved in commercial transactions that fall under the Uniform Commercial Code—as most business people are—you should become familiar with the UCC provisions in your state.

ASK YOURSELF

▶ Describe your business's policy about accepting checks. Include any specific provisions for attempting collection before requesting civil or criminal court assistance.

▶ Make sure everyone who collects funds for you understands this policy. You can even try to get them to agree to be liable for bad funds if they violate your check rules.

▶ Define your state's laws about bad checks.

▶ In what ways does the UCC apply to the kinds of commercial transactions your business or practice is involved in?

EMPLOYMENT LAW

LAWS FOR EMPLOYERS AND EMPLOYEES

Like so many other business dynamics, the relationship between employer and employee is created by contract. As we have seen with other contracts, the employment creation contract can be either *expressed* or *implied*.

Laws pertaining to the employer/employee relationship have evolved through judicial decision—the common law. Such laws have expanded primarily in subsets that involve contracts and torts. Employment law also involves federal statutes regarding labor and management. These laws apply to both union and nonunion workers and employers.

Federal law also comes into play when we discuss *constitutional* or *equal opportunity* issues, such as restrictions on employment based on sex, race, creed, age, national origin or physical abilities.

In employment issues, the first question is, *Who is the boss?*

The law assumes that within limits, the employer generally controls the employees' behavior, the work environment and workers' benefits.

The next question is, *Is the worker an agent of the boss?*

If the worker is an agent of the boss, it is possible for the agent to commit the employer—the boss—to liability. The employer could become bound to agreements or obligations made by the agent, even if the agent did not have the authority to create such an obligation; in fact, the employee may have acted in a manner exactly contrary to what his or her duties were as described by the employer—the boss.

Finally, both federal and state laws are involved when we discuss employee or workplace safety.

Let's look at some of the specific legal areas.

LABOR-MANAGEMENT LAW

Both federal and state laws cover the rights and obligations that arise out of the labor-management relationship.

In all states, certain federal statutes govern all labor management situations. Among the most significant federal laws to employers are:

Norris-LaGuardia Act

Passed in 1932, this law set up guidelines for management and labor disputes. It was intended to protect the status of unions as legitimate vehicles for employee concerns.

National Labor Relations Act (NLRA)

Enacted in 1935, NLRA gave legal legitimacy to unions. It became and remains the federal government's principal statutory support system for the philosophical concept of collective bargaining through unions. The NLRA defines certain actions that are considered unfair for management to do, including:

► Interference with employees' rights to unionize and/or to use the collective bargaining mechanism

► Attempts to dominate or control a union in violation of fair bargaining

► Attempts to discriminate against or to intimidate union members at work

► Attempts to discriminate against or to intimidate an employee who has exercised his or her rights under a collective bargaining agreement or under the NLRA

► Refuse to bargain in good faith with a designated representative of a union.

While some states also have laws governing unfair management practices, the federal laws have set the model for this relationship.

Labor-Management Reporting and Disclosure Act

Passed in 1959, this act created, in essence, a bill of rights for unions. The legislation attempts to bring greater democracy to union meetings and requires that unions make full disclosure of all relevant finances.

PROHIBITIONS AGAINST DISCRIMINATORY EMPLOYMENT PRACTICES

Similar to civil rights laws, these laws apply to all employees, whether or not the place of employment is unionized.

Equal Pay Act

This act:

- ▶ Prohibits every employer who has two or more employees from pay discrimination among those employees on the basis of sex

- ▶ Prohibits management from assigning different titles to two individuals who perform the same task

- ▶ Provides an avenue for an aggrieved employee who believes he or she has been discriminated against to seek back pay and an injunction

In addition, under this act, the Equal Employment Opportunity Commission (EEOC) has the authority to sue employers and to seek remedies.

Civil Rights Act of 1964

This act applies to all employers who have 15 or more employees. It prohibits discrimination based on race, color, sex, religion, physical capability and national origin.

This kind of discriminatory behavior had previously been prohibited by statute in many states. Beginning in 1964, employers nationwide also had to refrain from possible discrimination in firing, compensating, promoting and training employees, and from any other act that shows an adverse impact based on one of the prohibited factors under the Civil Rights Act.

Individual employees can also take action under this statute. The EEOC has the duty of enforcing this act; the Department of Justice represents the government's position in litigation.

The act acknowledges basic defenses that can be interposed by the alleged violator. If the employer uses a bona fide qualification system or a professionally developed ability test, or if there are bona fide occupational qualifications—not based on sex, race, national origin, creed, color or religion or any protected categories—the qualification system can be permitted. In such cases, the employer may justify the numerical results in his or her business and must be prepared to defend the reasons for the results.

Age Discrimination In Employment Act of 1967

This act prohibits discrimination in hiring, firing, compensation or otherwise, on the basis of age. Initially protecting employees between 40 and 65 years old, the age cap no longer exists.

The act prohibits mandatory retirement of employees; however, the employee may not be protected if job performance is affected.

Remedies may include:

▶ Back pay that was lost when an employee has been fired, when it turns out that such firing was not proper

▶ Back pay in the amount the employee would have earned had the employee received a promotion for which he or she is qualified

Remedies can also include injunctive relief and the requirement for affirmative action.

If your company has 20 or more employees—including part-time employees—find out about possible responsibilities under this act.

The Americans with Disabilities Act

This historic statute specifies certain rights and remedies for people with disabilities. It covers the workplace as well as other locations. For people who claim discrimination based on physical ability, this act has the practical effect of adding to the Civil Rights Act. More information on the Americans with Disabilities Act is included below, under Americans With Disabilities.

WAGE FAIRNESS AND FAIR LABOR STANDARDS

These laws govern wage parity and working conditions. The laws are presented by enforcement level—federal and state.

The Federal Law

The Fair Labor Standards Act (FLSA) covers workers in interstate commerce and workers providing goods in interstate commerce. It establishes minimum wage rates for regular time, overtime rates, equal pay, record-keeping rules and standards for child labor.

▶ *Wage and Hour Controls.* The FLSA contains certain provisions that dictate requirements for an employee's wages and hours.

▶ *Employers Affected.* The wage and hour law is enforced through the commerce power of the federal government; it applies to any employer whose activity or output affects interstate commerce or who is in interstate commerce.

The generally accepted presumption regarding virtually all federal laws where interstate commerce is the jurisdictional basis for federal action is that most manufactured, imported or exported goods affect interstate commerce.

The FLSA sets minimum rates of pay and determines when an employer must pay. It also restricts child labor and contains civil liabilities and criminal penalties for violations.

The FLSA presents an array of enforcement possibilities, including:

▶ Criminal prosecution, including fine and imprisonment

▶ Injunctive proceedings—as part of which the Secretary of Labor may also seek unpaid wages

- Wage damage suits that provide a legal mechanism for employees to collect double unpaid wages, plus costs and attorney's fees

- Wage suits by the Secretary of Labor on behalf of the employee

- Supervision of payment of past due wages by the Wage-Hour Administrator, who is empowered by the act with the statutory power to prescribe record-keeping requirements

State Wage-Hour Laws

In addition to federal laws, many states have enacted legislation on minimum wages, maximum hours and child labor. While federal laws predominate state laws under general principles of federalism, in the labor and wage area, states are not preempted from enacting legislation with higher standards than the federal government's. In fact, most states had legislation in these areas before the federal government got into the labor law business.

Americans with Disabilities (ADA)

The ADA was enacted to prohibit discrimination in the workplace, based on physical disability.

ADA covers two major areas.

- Prevention of discrimination against workers with physical or mental disabilities—as long as they are able to do the job or a comparable job

- Requiring accommodation for people, including workers with supported environments.

Since the ADA is so new, there is still some confusion around the Act's requirements for employers. Most state labor departments, the U.S. Department of Justice and Equal Opportunity Commission and the President's Committee on People with Disabilities in Washington, D.C., can provide valuable guidance.

For more information, an excellent booklet is *The Americans with Disabilities Act*, also known as the "little yellow booklet." It is available from local offices of the EEOC and from the Department of Justice.[10]

Sexual Harassment

Sexual harassment cases usually involve actions by males directed at females, but apply equally to both genders.

Complaints frequently take one of three forms.

- ► Requiring submission to sexual advances as a condition for employment
- ► Retaliation against the employee for resisting unwelcome sexual advances
- ► Activities by which the employer or its employees create an offensive atmosphere that interferes with job performance

If an employee charges an employer or co-worker with harassment, the result is always unpleasant, even if the allegations are not sustained. While sexual harassment cases are often well publicized, they are not necessarily easy for the plaintiff to win, and the defendant is certainly tainted by the charges.

The best solution for sexual harassment is to prevent it. Employers must have increased sensitivity to gender-based issues and, if necessary, train their workers to avoid the allegation, rather than have to defend against it.[11]

---

10. See also *Americans With Disabilities Act* by Mary B. Dickson, Crisp Publications, 1993.

11. See also *Sexual Harassment in the Workplace: A Guide to Prevention* by Juliana Lightle, Ph.D. and Elizabeth H. Doucet, Crisp Publications, 1992.

EMPLOYEE SAFETY AND WORKING CONDITIONS

Both the state and federal government have enacted laws and departmental regulations designed to provide workers with a relatively safe and healthy working environment. Most of these laws rose out of general exploitation of workers by management and some highly visible tragedies that took place in the United States in the early years of the industrial revolution. One such tragedy was the Triangle Shirtwaist Company factory fire in New York City in 1911, which killed 145 workers, all of them women and girls.

The Occupational Safety and Health Act is the most significant law on the topic.

Occupational Safety and Health Act

The federal government did not enact the first major national federal safety statute that applied to most businesses until 1970. Until then, workplace safety regulation depended on local laws and regulations or specific industry coverage, such as mine safety laws.

Occupational Safety and Health Act requirements apply to all businesses that affect interstate commerce; while a business must have a minimum number of employees for the Act to apply, the commerce concept can be stretched to cover virtually all employers. In fact, court decisions support the premise that the Occupational Safety and Health Act affects virtually all businesses.

Since the Occupational Safety and Health Act is a police power statute, it does not create a private cause of action for an employee. This means an employee cannot sue the employer directly for noncompliance; however, since the government could close the business down or fine it, this Act has strong teeth.

The Occupational Safety and Health Act is aimed at protecting the safety, health and welfare of employees by:

- Creating a certain minimal duty for covered employers to prevent workplace hazards that could cause serious injury or death to employees

- Delegating to the Secretary of Labor the authority to establish health and safety standards with which employers must comply.

Certain minimum levels of exposure to hazardous substances may be established by regulation. These have included levels of asbestos, lead and other toxic chemicals. Employers who require work that is dangerous or that involves materials that could be hazardous to health must comply. Compliance can impose such wide-ranging mechanisms as ear plugs for airport workers to back braces for people who do heavy lifting.[12]

One of the effects of the Occupational Safety and Health Act was to establish three new federal agencies.

- The Occupational Safety and Health Administration (OSHA)

- The National Institute of Occupational Safety and Health (NIOSH)

- The Occupational Safety and Health Review Commission

OSHA, the best known of the three agencies, is located within the Department of Labor.

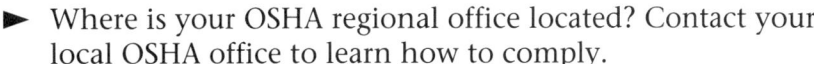

Your Turn

Please answer the following questions:

- Where is your OSHA regional office located? Contact your local OSHA office to learn how to comply.

- List the safety hazards in your work environment.

- Are you aware of OSHA requirements that apply to working with the material(s) your firm uses?

---

12. See also *A Manager's Guide to OSHA* by Neville C. Tompkins, Crisp Publications, 1993.

Both state and federal agencies are very serious about violations of health and safety workplace laws—and they both may have the power to close your business down.

Providing a safe and healthy environment is not only the moral thing to do, it is also good business. The healthiest, happiest employees are the best employees.

EMPLOYMENT BENEFITS

You may be surprised to know how knowledgeable employees are about benefits that could be provided to them in a small business.

Generally speaking, most medical care, including insured health benefits, is not counted as income to the employee. In addition, other benefits such as pension or profit-sharing plans, cafeteria plans, group legal service plans and dependent care assistance can usually be provided with similar tax exemptions.

Employee benefit programs have tax implications; some of these benefits need not be included in the gross income of the employees who receive them.

There are limits on the amount of benefits that certain shareholders and owner-employees can receive.

Employee Benefits

▶ **Tax-Qualified Plans of Deferred Compensation**

These include stock bonus, pension or profit-sharing plans provided by the employer—which must be for the exclusive benefit of the employees and their beneficiaries. These plans must meet specific requirements of the Internal Revenue Code.

Examples of these kinds of plans are:

• *Pension Plans:* These plans are established and maintained by employers to provide benefits to the employee over a period of years after retirement. Pension plans must be definitely determinable; that is, the basis for determining what financial resources go into the plan must be specific.

The plans can also provide fixed contributions each year by the employers on behalf of the employees. Pension plans can provide benefits that are in addition to the retirement benefits, such as disability or death benefits.

- *Annuity Plans:* The major difference between pension and annuity plans is that annuity plan resources are paid out of annuity or insurance contracts.

- *Profit-Sharing Plans:* These plans are established and maintained by employers. They are funded from profits—if any—earned by the employer and shared with employees.

- *Stock Bonus Plans:* Established and maintained by the employer, these plans provide benefits similar to those of profit-sharing plans; however, benefits and the contributions are derived from the appreciation—if any—in the value of shares and/or the dividends or income from stocks, rather than from the employer's profits.

- *Cash or Deferred Plans*: Also known as *Section 401(K) Plans* under the Internal Revenue Code, these plans permit employees to have their salary reduced on a pre-tax basis and invested in a profit sharing, fixed contribution or stock bonus plan. IRS regulations must be monitored carefully for employees under these plans.

Medical Benefits for Employees, Retirees and Spouses

An employer can provide medical benefits, including a pension or annuity plan that provides for the payment of benefits for sickness, accident, health and medical expenses of employees, retired employees, spouses and dependents, if certain conditions are met.

▶ Cafeteria Plans

Cafeteria plans offer some variability in the employee's choice of benefits. A plan may allow employees to place a certain amount of money into one or more medical plans; a medical plan and a dental plan or a medical plan, dental plan and employee dependent care coverage.

▶ Other benefits can include such items as:

- Qualified group legal service plans
- Dependent care assistance programs
- Employee maternity leave plans

Your Turn   *Please answer the following questions:*

▶ Do you have a knowledgeable employee benefits consultant or attorney or tax consultant who is familiar with the tax implications of the various employee benefit options?

▶ Is a cafeteria plan something your employees would benefit from?

- If so, have you considered establishing a cafeteria plan?

WORKERS' COMPENSATION LAWS

Some years ago, the law left unanswered questions about workers' abilities to sue employers for injuries that occurred to them while at work. Equity and fairness required something to be done that would provide recourse to employees hurt on the job.

A new theory arose which established *absolute liability* by the employer for injury or illness to workers. Absolute liability means that fault is not an issue.

All states have now enacted workers' compensation acts. These laws create commissions and boards to determine if an injured employee is entitled to receive compensation.

One of the benefits to the employee is that, unlike negligence cases, there are virtually no defenses to an employee's recovery for being injured on the job. This absolute liability theory is true even if the employee or a fellow employee is responsible.

Under workers' compensation laws, the employee will be compensated in most states by the mere fact of the injury.

To compensate for the absolute liability of these laws, every state has a limitation on the amount of compensation the employee will receive. Recovery usually includes medical expenses reasonably related to the injury. Employees can receive this compensation as long as they were injured in the course of normal employment activities. The tribunal, if contested issues arise, is a state board. Generally, courts only enter the picture to review decisions of these boards or commissions.

Amounts recoverable by an employee are fixed by statute for a particular type of injury. Recovery for injuries under workers' compensation laws are generally less than the common-law recovery would have been, if the worker had been allowed by law to sue for negligence.

If a third party—other than the employer or fellow employees—is responsible for the injury, the employee can bring a tort action against that party or file a workers' compensation action. Normally, the worker cannot recover in full from both the employer and a third party.

The theory behind workers' compensation laws is to provide income replacement, medical care and rehabilitation services for workers who have job-related injuries or sicknesses. These laws can also provide income benefits for survivors of employees whose deaths were job-related.

FEDERAL INCOME SECURITY PROTECTION

If an employee's family loses earnings as a result of death, disability, retirement or medical expenses, the family may be entitled to compensation under the Social Security Act (SSA).

As part of the national citizen welfare program, Congress created Social Security in 1935, to provide limited retirement and death benefits for certain covered employees. Since then, additional features have been added to the original act, including:

▶ Old age and survivor's insurance

▶ Disability insurance

▶ Hospitalization insurance (Medicare)

▶ Supplemental security income, based on need

As everyone who has ever received a paycheck knows, funds for the Social Security system come from "contributions" from employers and employees and from self-employed individuals. Usually, employees and employers pay matching contributions. The percentage of contribution and benefits change occasionally, but not necessarily on an annual basis.

The employer is obligated to make sure the employee's portion of the taxes is withheld. The employer remits these payments to the Internal Revenue Service on a periodic basis, along with other taxes. The employee's contributions are not tax deductible by the employer; however, amounts contributed to Social Security by the employer are tax deductible by the employer.

UNEMPLOYMENT INSURANCE

The Federal Unemployment Insurance System was created in 1935, as part of the Social Security Act. Later, particular provisions of the SSA were supplemented by the Federal Unemployment Tax Act and other federal laws. These laws, as well as state laws, provide a method of covering unemployment.

Unemployment coverage applies only under specific conditions. Under the joint federal and state program, workers discharged without being at fault can receive unemployment compensation. Each state has its own approach and different unemployment compensation level. States usually require an employee to have worked a minimum period or to have earned a minimum wage amount to qualify for coverage.

The periods, amounts and length of benefits vary by state. The unemployed worker must be ready and able to accept new employment to receive unemployment compensation.

ASK YOURSELF

▶ Describe your current and planned benefit programs. Be sure to assess your employee morale needs and financial capability in your answer.

▶ Draft the personnel policies and procedures that would benefit your firm.

THE AGENT
OF YOUR
BUSINESS

WHAT IS AN AGENT?

Any person—or organization—who acts on behalf of another may be considered the *agent* of the person—or organization—who invites such action. This simplistic statement introduces an important concept in business law.

The idea of someone entering into a contract on behalf of someone else may be a little disconcerting; however, in many contexts, it is the way we do business. If I ask my secretary to go to the stationery store to buy a box of file folders and charge it to my account, I cannot later refuse to pay because I, personally, did not buy them.

As a practical matter, virtually every organization needs the ability to designate someone to act legally on its behalf. Because of the unique nature of this type of person's relationship to the organization and the fact that these people seem to conduct business on behalf of the organization, the law has created a distinct group of rules governing their conduct.

This niche within the law arose out of the need, on the part of people dealing with organizations, to be able to rely upon the ability of the other people to engage in binding relationships or agreements. Known as the *law of agency*, rules of law and industry practice dictate what a person may or may not do to bind the organization on whose behalf the agent acts—or appears to act.

This chapter goes beyond the law of contracts and the legal issues that surround employment; it focuses on relationships that often exist in business, which rise out of contracts, but which fall short of officer- and director-binding relationships. These relationships concern the people who act on behalf of businesses and organizations, and who may or may not be employees.

This chapter discusses the need for a company to assign representatives to act legally in its behalf, as the rules of agency law which govern such action. The perspective is of the person or organization who creates the agency relationship and from the person or organization who deals with people they expect and may even assume to be acting at the official behest of the organization.

HOW THE AGENCY RELATIONSHIP IS CREATED

The relationship between principal and agent is created in one of four ways.

▶ The principal specifically appoints the agent to act for him or her.

▶ The principal advises others that the agent has been appointed.

▶ The principal may become liable for additional acts of the agent after the agent was given original authority—if the principal knew or should have known that the agent had apparent authority to act.

▶ The principal ratifies—legally approves—the acts of the person acting on his or her behalf, even though the principal had not authorized such acts in advance.

The principal-agent relationship may sometimes arise by operation of law—statute—where the state has a legislative need to create an automatic agency rule. For example:

▶ The so-called *family purpose doctrine*, which is law in many states, presumes that a member of a family who is operating a vehicle is doing so for family purposes and is, therefore, an agent for the family.

▶ Relevant to doing business in a state other than one's own, many states have laws creating the Secretary of State as the agent for service of process—that is, the person on whom legal documents can be served upon the institution of legal proceedings—within their state, against companies from other jurisdictions—foreign corporations. Therefore, companies doing business in a state where they are not incorporated must select and report an agent for the firm to receive the legal process. Otherwise, the state presumes the Secretary of State has been designated.

In short, agency relationships are created by the parties themselves or, in limited circumstances, by a state acting to protect its citizens from potentially confusing situations.

Please answer the following questions:

► List the four ways the relationship between the principal and agent can be created.

1. _____

2. _____

3. _____

4. _____

AGENCY IN ACTION

How do these theories apply to the real world of business?

Envision a situation where person or organization A needs person or organization B to act on A's behalf. B may or may not be an employee. The hiring entity is known as the *principal*. The hired entity—B in this example—is known as the *agent*.

A key element in the test for agency is what power the agent has to bind the principal. If a person or firm has created the agency—authorized the agent to act—acts taken by the agent while in this capacity bind the principal. If the agent has not been authorized to act, or if the action is beyond the scope of employment, the action might not bind the principal.

So the rule is that agents can bind principals as long as the agents are acting within their authority to act, which is the power given to them by the principals. Contracts entered into by agents acting with proper authority are as binding as those entered into by principals acting for themselves.

Determining what actions and persons can bind a principal is critical to smooth business dealing. If the principal could back out of a deal he or she does not like by claiming the agent was not authorized, no one would do business with anyone other than owners or duly authorized officers or directors of firms. Business and commerce would be brought to a stop.

On the other hand, must the employer or principal always be bound by what the employee or agent does?

If this is true, no one would hire anyone else or allow anyone to do anything that might lead to potential liability. Such an attitude would also adversely affect commerce.

Your Turn

Please answer the following questions:

▶ Who is the principal of your company?

▶ Who are the agents of your company?

- _____
- _____
- _____
- _____
- _____
- _____

How the Law Finds the Middle Ground

The test is the legal concept of *reasonableness*. In agency law, reasonableness applies to the conduct of both principal and agent.

▶ If the action taken by the principal manifests an expressed intention to create an agency relationship, then agency exists.

▶ If the language or action taken did not expressly create the agency relationship, but such action was reasonably designed to create the expectation that an agency relationship exists, then it exists.

The latter theory, known as *implied agency*, is similar to the difference between creation of an express or implied contract.

The *inherent agency* relationship is the third and final type of agency relationships. In inherent agency-principal relationships, the agent has the authority to take certain action from the nature of the assignment itself.

For example, a police officer does not seek permission of his or her supervisor to make a routine arrest. Police officers have the inherent authority to take such action because they are sworn officers. Presumably the decision will be reviewed at some point by a principal—that is, a higher authority in the department.

In addition to governing the creation of the agency relationship, the law of agency governs the rights, duties and liabilities of agents and principals. The general rule is that the agent has the duty of good faith and loyalty to his or her principal. In some states, this duty is elevated to a fiduciary relationship—one of special trust. Normally, the agent is not personally liable for contracts entered into on behalf of his or her principal. An agent can become personally liable if he or she exceeds the authority.

CASE STUDY

Biff, the Greeter

Biff was hired as a greeter at a night club; an ex-lineman for an NFL football team, he makes an imposing figure at the doorway. The owner told him he is to keep underage people out and to help maintain order inside the premises.

A customer gets nasty and drunk inside the premises. The owner asks Biff to request that the drunken customer leave.

Biff approaches the customer and asks him politely to leave.

The customer then makes a unpleasant remark about Biff's family lineage; Biff loses his temper and hits the man, causing serious injury.

Is the owner liable in damages for Biff's act?

This is not an easy case. Biff's attack on the customer is considered an intentional tort. The standard rule is that principals are not liable for the intentional torts of agents; the principal is liable for the reasonable acts of the agent in the course of his employment.

Is injuring a customer part of the course of employment?

The answer depends upon the instructions that the owner gave Biff.

- ▶ If the owner told Biff he was never to strike a customer on any occasion and that by doing so, he—Biff—would be responsible for the outcome, the owner might be off the hook.

- ▶ If the customer assumes Biff struck him as part of Biff's employment, and if the customer's assumption was reasonably based on the facts, then the owner may be legally liable under the theory of *apparent agency*.

- ▶ If the owner knew Biff had a nasty temper or short fuse, Biff's act could be imputed to the owner, who could be liable even though he never gave Biff permission to do what he did.

The apparent agency theory reasons that it is up to the owner to make clear that Biff is an independent contractor, not an agent, and that as an independent contractor, Biff is liable for his own acts.

This same theory applies in the contract area: if an agent exceeds authority while negotiating a deal for the principal, he or she can bind the principal, if the principal knew or should have known about the agent's acts.

When asking an agent to do something, the safest road is to make it clear to both the agent and to those persons working with him or her that the person is either not an employee or is not authorized to bind the principal.

The independent contractor relationship is an example of delineating clearly the working arrangement. Again review the sample form for Independent Contractor, Exhibit 6 in Appendix I.

Independent contractors are not agents of the principal. They are people or organizations who have contracted fully for a particular service. As such, they are liable for their own acts and cannot hide behind the principals. To protect the public when they are working with independent contractors, it should be made clear that the person/firm is a contractor and not an agent for the principal.

The law uses several tests to differentiate between an agent and an independent contractor. These include:

▶ *The basis for compensation:* Agents are usually paid on a regular basis—for example, salary or draw. Contractors are paid a particular sum for a particular task.

▶ *The measure of control:* An agent's work on the task is controlled by the principal. A contractor maintains complete control of her or her own tasks.

▶ *Who supplies materials and tools:* Most agents use tools and materials supplied by the principal. Contractors usually furnish their own materials and tools.

► *The nature of the work—the calling:* This test relies on the generalizations or presumptions common to the *calling* of the person. Therefore, domestic servants, chauffeurs, gardeners and *au pair* assistants would usually be agents. Painters, plumbers and electricians would usually be independent contractors.

Please note: Every test is based on generalizations and creates only presumptions of either agency or independent contractor status. Other factors can be developed to either support or rebut this presumption.

Why is all this so important?

The worker's legal status dictates who shall be legally liable for contracts and other acts of the person.

► If the worker is an agent, the principal is liable.

► If the worker is an independent contractor, the worker may be liable.

Let's visit The Laura Little Studio for an example that illustrates why the potential of liability for the acts of another person is so important.

CASE STUDY

Update on Laura's Business

In expanding her business, Laura hired both employees and artists who work as independent contractors. On the same day she hired Sarah at a weekly salary, she asked Jay to write some ad copy as an independent contractor.

The agency was so busy that Laura decided to keep Jay on indefinitely as an independent contractor. She paid him his gross earnings on an hourly basis without deductions for taxes, hospitalization or anything else.

Sarah's paycheck reflected the standard deductions as an employee. After about a month, Sarah became frustrated working at the temporary table set-up she had been supplied. She went to Laura and requested a new table and chair; Laura told her to order the furniture. Sarah contacted an art supply house, asked them to deliver the merchandise and had them bill The Laura Little Studio.

Jay had been writing his ad copy on an old personal computer that he owned and had brought to the studio from his home. He became frustrated when other programs he was using would not interface with the updated computers used at The Laura Little Studio. Jay went to a neighborhood computer store and ordered a new notebook computer that would interface with the Studio's equipment. He told the store to invoice The Laura Little Studio.

Jay took the computer back to the Studio where he began to do some great, creative work. Some evenings, he took the new computer home, where he would continue to work on a project; and sometimes he used it to work on his own short stories.

At the end of the month, two invoices arrived at The Laura Little Studio. Laura approved the expenditure and signed the check for the art supply store to pay for Sarah's new table and chair. She did not, however, approve the expenditure to the computer store for Jay's new computer.

When the computer store contacted Laura, she told them that her firm had not purchased the equipment; Jay had made the purchase and Jay was liable for payment.

Jay was upset and told Laura that he bought the equipment to use for the Studio, not for himself; he admitted that he had used the new computer for nonbusiness purposes, but that he had never billed The Laura Little Studio for his personal time on the computer.

Who should pay for the computer Jay has been using?

The answer to this question is not easy. The test for legal liability will consider the four factors that differentiate an agent and an independent contractor. It will also take into account the perspective of the seller of the merchandise at the computer store.

► Did the retailer think that Jay was acting on behalf of The Laura Little Studio and that Jay was entitled reasonably to do so?

► As an independent contractor, wasn't Jay supposed to supply the tools he needed for his work?

► In truth, hadn't Laura asked Jay to stay on indefinitely?

► Didn't Jay need adequate tools to produce his work?

► Didn't The Laura Little Studio receive the benefit of having the computer?

The answer to who would be liable depends upon whether or not Jay had sought permission in advance to purchase the equipment. If so, he would have become an authorized agent to purchase the merchandise; if not, he was unauthorized and the only way the firm could be liable is if they failed to take appropriate action to prevent a misunderstanding. However, the computer store should have checked with the Studio to verify that Jay was authorized to bind them.

The answer becomes even less clear when one considers the fact that the Studio has the benefit of using the equipment. If Jay left the device at work when he was not there and other people used it, the Studio may have *ratified* Jay's unauthorized act.

Based on the limited facts presented here, the computer is Jay's own equipment and he has to pay. If the computer store has a problem collecting, they will have to find recourse through Jay.

WHAT ACTS CAN BIND THE PRINCIPAL?

THE GENERAL RULE

As a principal, you will be bound by the authorized acts of agents. You can be bound by unauthorized acts if you have not taken precise steps to:

► Limit the legal authority and

► Inform people working with that agent of that fact.

> **This generalization should be a warning to you to be clear with employees, agents, independent contractors, clients and customers about who has your permission to do what. You must know what people are saying and doing on your behalf outside your shop.**

ASK YOURSELF

► Identify the areas in your business dealings and relationships where an agency relationship exists.

► Discuss the steps you have taken to protect yourself from being bound to acts of agents by any confusion that you might have created.

► What is your understanding of your relationships with representatives of other firms and organizations that you know, as to whether or not they have the authority to work with you to suit your purposes?

PROTECTING BUSINESS INTELLECTUAL PROPERTY

PROTECT YOUR IDEAS

Business could not survive without a mechanism to protect new ideas, trade secrets, processes, designs, writings and other works that represent the products of creative minds and intellects. *Intellectual property law*, a subset of commercial law, is the field of law that covers the legal protection of innovations.

Intellectual property law is very technical and invites the assistance of a lawyer specially versed in the particular topic. Practitioners are commonly specialists who have backgrounds in both the law and the technical area of innovation. Some important general knowledge about the field is necessary for any person involved in a business or profession that relies upon research and development or other innovative thinking that is aimed at offering a new or distinctive product or service.

If your business meets any of these criteria, be sure you know the opportunities and mechanisms for protecting your property rights and be aware of your obligations not to infringe on the legal rights of others.

Intellectual property law involves a compendium of federal and state laws, administrative regulations and court decisions. The following general outline identifies the individual areas of intellectual property law.

PATENT PROTECTION

What Is Patent Protection?

The founders of this country felt that the population needed encouragement to develop a robust economy. One early concept for new business stimulation allowed those who conceptualized new ideas to establish a legal monopoly. Their concept may have worked, since the United States has consistently been a base for major innovation and invention in the world economy.

Our patent system is based upon this notion. A patent is the legal means by which a government grants to an inventor a *statutory monopoly*—in the United States, this amounts to 17 years—for any "new and useful process, machine, manufacture, or composition of matter, or any new and useful improvement thereof." Certain unique and distinctive designs can also receive a patent.

Design patents give *ornamental protection* for three-and-a-half, seven or 14 years; the applicant chooses the time frame. The patent grant prohibits anyone else from practicing the invention or using the design for the life of the patent; anyone who infringes can be found in violation of both civil and criminal prohibitions.

What Is Patentable and Who Can Get a Patent?

Patents protect innovative ideas. According to the Patent Act, patent protection is available for:

- ▶ Processes
- ▶ Machines
- ▶ Manufacturing process
- ▶ Composition of matter, including chemical formulae
- ▶ "New and useful" improvements

In recent years, patents have also been issued for plants, certain software algorithms and genetically engineered animals.

These categories are often referred to as the subject matter of patents. In addition to being appropriate subject matter, the invention must be:

- ▶ *Useful.* Over the years, this has been construed to mean "having some utilitarian value."

- ▶ *Reduced to practice.* This means that the Patent and Trademark Office (PTO) Examiner must be able to see that the invention is more than pure theory; it must be capable of being produced. Therefore, without building the full-sized bridge, the concept for a new bridge could be patented if the inventor demonstrated, through a model or otherwise, that the invention could be practiced—used.

► *New.* That means it cannot have been used before and it cannot have been published, since that would put it into the public domain. This requirement is strict. For example, if a professor develops a new theory and publishes a paper about it, the theory is no longer new, and a patent, if applied for, will not be granted.

► *Created by the person who applies for the patent.* There is an important distinction here between assignability of the patent once issued and assignability of the right to apply. It is considered fraudulent conduct for an inventor to transfer an idea to someone else who then applies for the patent; consequences for fraudulent conduct are far worse than mere rejection of the patent application.

If there is a need to assign the rights, it is done after the inventor applies for the patent and is available to pursue the application.

In short, to obtain a patent, the following minimum requirements must be met. The invention should:

► Be appropriate subject matter for a patent

► Have a utilitarian value

► Be able to be reduced to practice

► Be novel

► Be invented by the applicant

While meeting all of these requirements allows the application process to proceed, it does not guarantee that a patent will be issued.

How to Apply for a Patent

The PTO maintains forms and procedures for proper application. It is possible to prepare and file your own application, but obtaining the services of a patent attorney or agent is strongly encouraged.

The application process involves the following basic steps:

► Prepare and file the appropriate application and pay the necessary filing fees.

► The file—referred to by patent attorneys as *case*—is assigned to a PTO examiner. That examiner's job is to review the materials and compare them with earlier patents and other materials—known as *prior art.*

► The PTO responds with a report of the initial review. The response is often a rejection that states the relevant grounds.

► The applicant—usually through counsel—files an amended application with the changes as defined in the report of the initial review.

► The application is granted a letters patent with a number and certificate—or it may be rejected again for further work.

During the time when the application is filed and when the patent is granted, the applicant is permitted to use the term *Patent Pending*. This important provision gives the public notice that an application for protection has been made to the PTO. To prevent abuse of this process, the law calls for a fine for misuse of the term *Patent Pending;* presumably, this dissuades infringement.

Assuming that a patent is granted, let's look at what the inventor gets with a patent.

The Nature of the Rights in a Patent

A patent is not an exclusive permission to practice the patent. Instead, it prohibits people, other than the duly registered inventors to practice the invention.

In other words, a patent gives the inventor the right to stop someone else from violating this statutory monopoly. This type of violation is called an *infringement.*

As you have seen, the issuance of a patent does not automatically grant the inventor permission to use the technology to make something. Suppose that you developed a new formula for a type of insecticide that was not permitted under current environmental laws; even if you were issued a patent, you could not practice it without complying with other legal requirements.

Patents are available only to inventions the inventor did not *abandon*. Here, abandonment means that the inventor fails to pursue patent application rights within a reasonable amount of time. This can be shown by an express act by the inventor or it can be implied from his or her conduct.

Enforcing Legal Rights

It would seem as if the right to exclusively practice an invention through a patent ought to be clear and without confusion. After all, before a patent issues, a highly qualified examiner, who is usually familiar with other items that are available in the field, reviews the case and decides whether or not a patent should be allowed.

Each year the PTO receives more applications from all over the world than any one examiner can realistically keep track of; if an examiner is not aware of another, identical invention, he or she will recommend that a patent be granted.

Infringement refers to the unlawful usurpation of an individual—or firm's—exclusive rights to commercially exploit or otherwise practice the invention. Infringement can take a number of forms. It usually involves copying or otherwise *ripping off* or *knocking off* a patented product, without permission to do so.

Infringement can be domestic—from within the United States—or it can be foreign—non-U.S. manufactured goods that violate patent rights entering the United States.

You have two options if you believe your patent has been infringed:

► You can seek an injunction.

► You can sue for damages.

Great care and good legal advice are strongly advised before any decision is made to respond to allegations of patent infringement. Suits under the patent laws are brought in federal district courts; both remedies are often requested as alternatives in a federal patent infringement suit.

Direct applications for foreign infringements are made to the United States Trade Commission in Washington, D.C. That agency can issue an order to exclude a product from entry into the United States.

Often, suits alleging patent infringement are responded to with allegations that the patent is not valid—that is, the patent should never have been issued. Sometimes, these counterclaims prevail and the original patentee—patent holder—loses all patent protection.

Some attorneys and other commentators refer to a patent as nothing more than a "fighting interest in a lawsuit." Whether or not this is true, if the infringer has the resources to countersue, the litigation may not be worth engaging in.

Patent owners often consider granting licenses to alleged infringers as part of the process of enforcing the rights. At the least, under this model there will be some financial consideration for the infringement.

A former corporate client of mine refused to grant a license to a Taiwanese firm that wanted to manufacture a popular tool sold on U.S. television. My client's U.S. patent did not deter the rejected Taiwanese company from knocking off the product. We eventually stopped them, but by then they had sold as much product as my client had sold and they had gone out of business in the United States. Our victory, which cost my client many thousands of dollars, was important as a warning to others, but was empty in financial terms.

If enforcing patents is so expensive and may not result in a positive outcome, why bother to get a patent?

Many firms do not get patents. They just hope to get to the market first and use quality and advertising as their resources for their market share. Other firms, especially larger firms with in-house patent counsel and/or substantial financial resources, are prepared to fight to prevent infringement.

If you have developed a distinctive and potentially patentable product, you will need to weigh the advantages against the costs and other disadvantages before you decide whether or not to apply for a patent. By all means, seek competent legal advice before applying for a patent.

Your Turn

Please answer the following questions:

► What are the five requirements to get a patent?

1. _____

2. _____

3. _____

4. _____

5. _____

► What are the rules regarding *patent pending*?

► What action can be taken against infringement?

COPYRIGHT PROTECTION OF PROPERTY

A copyright protects the manifestation of an idea, not the idea itself. If an author writes a book, the ideas expressed in the book are not protected, but rather the actual words, phrases and structure—the physical manifestation of the book idea—receive copyright protection.

COPYRIGHT PROTECTION

Based on federal laws, copyright protection gives the owner exclusive rights to:

► Reproduce and distribute the protected work

► Prepare a derived work based on the copyright protected original

► Publicly perform or display the copyrighted work

How to Obtain Copyright Protection

Application for copyright protection is made on Form TX, available from the Register of Copyrights, Copyright Office, The Library of Congress, Washington D.C. 20559.

The Register of Copyrights is responsible for copyright protection. When a form is filed, together with the appropriate fee and two copies of the work, the copyright is presumed to have been issued.

Unlike patent application, copyright applications are not subject to extensive review, searches and clearances. In essence, review is made only when there is an allegation by another person that a copyright should not be issued. Grounds for objecting to an application for copyright include allegations that:

► The applied-for work infringes upon someone else's rights

► The author claimed is not the real author

To symbolize your copyright protection and comply with some of the international copyright conventions, notice of your copyright claim should be uniform. The suggested form is the symbol © or the word *Copyright*, followed by the year of creation and the name of the owner. Although it is not legally required, you can also add the phrase:

All rights reserved

I use these words as further evidence of my determination to protect my rights. For example, the following identifies my written materials:

According to the Copyright Act of January 1, 1978, the term of protection commences when the work is created and continues for the life of the author, plus 50 years. For works for hire, where someone is asked to create something under contract, the term is 75 years or 100 years from creation, whichever is shorter. Thereafter, as with patent ideas, the copyright reverts to the public domain.

There is an important distinction between the way patents and copyrights are derived. In patents, a formal application must be made before protection or legal rights enure. This is not so with copyrights. The rights begin upon the creation of the work.

In fact, one never needs to apply for a federal copyright to have a copyright. The so-called *common law copyright* gives the author the right to stop anyone else from taking his or her copyrighted materials. State courts can be used for these personal rights.

Of course, proving the case might be quite difficult. By filing with the Copyright Office, the copyright holder receives access to federal courts and some documentation of his or her rights. Once in federal court, the copyright owner can have attorneys fees paid and even seek punishment against an intentional infringer.

Who Owns the Copyright?

This question poses problems for the general public, as well as for practitioners of intellectual property law. The question becomes even more difficult if an outsider is hired to create a work for remuneration.

A landmark 1989 U.S. Supreme Court decision relating to the U.S. Copyright Act's "work made for hire" provisions is *Community for Creative Non-Violence,* (CCNV) *et al. v. Reid*, No. 88-293 (June 5, 1989). This case confirms the importance of using carefully prepared written assignment agreements with both independent contractors and with employees who are engaged in creative development services.

Although the work in this case was a copyrightable work—a work of art—any assignment you or your attorney prepare should also cover all types of intellectual property rights.

Unfortunately, in the CCNV case, the Supreme Court did not create clear criteria for when someone is considered an employee, but left that to a subjective test on a case-by-case basis. This means that litigation over ownership of a newly developed work could arise when there is no agreement delineating such rights, particularly in the independent contractor situation. As a practical matter, the only way a company can be assured that it owns the work product of an independent contractor is based upon a formal written assignment agreement.

Let's look at "Work Made for Hire Provisions" of the United States Copyright Act. Section 101 defines a "work made for hire" as:

1. a work prepared by an employee within the scope of his or her employment; or

2. a work specially ordered or commissioned for use
   a. as a contribution to a collective work,
   b. as a part of a motion picture or other audiovisual work,
   c. as a translation,
   d. as a supplementary work,
   e. as a compilation,
   f. as an instructional text,
   g. as a test,
   h. as answer material for a test, or
   i. as an atlas,

if the parties expressly agree in a written instrument signed by them that the work shall be considered a work made for hire.

Section 201(b) of the Act provides that, for copyright purposes, the employer or other person for whom a work made for hire was prepared is considered the author of the work.

Under Section 101, to qualify as a "work made for hire," a work must either be prepared by an employee within the ordinary scope of employment under agency rules, or must fall into one of the categories of commissioned works *and* be subject to a written agreement between the parties that the work is to be classified as a work made for hire.

Different interpretations of the meaning of "employee" have emerged in the case law. Several courts adopted what they call a literal interpretation. Under the strictest version of the so-called literal interpretation, to be an employee, the party creating the work must be a legitimate, salaried employee of the party requesting that the work be prepared.

Under the second major interpretation, courts have construed the word employee to include more than just formal salaried employees within agency law rules. Under this theory, even an independent contractor could be considered an employee if the independent contractor "were sufficiently supervised and directed by the hiring party."

The Supreme Court decision in the CCNV case raises serious questions about the ability to engage in creative work and applicability of the so-called "works for hire" provision. This case is not only significant but also interesting. It is worth taking a closer look at.

In 1985, Community for Creative Non-Violence, et al. entered into an oral agreement with Reid, a sculptor, to produce a statue dramatizing the plight of the homeless. After the statue was completed and delivered, the parties filed competing copyright registration certificates. No mention of copyright rights was made in the agreement between Reid and CCNV. The federal district court held the sculpture was a "work made for hire" of an *employee* and, therefore, was owned exclusively by CCNV.

The U.S. Court of Appeals reversed the federal district court's decision, holding that the sculpture was not a "work made for hire," since it was not "prepared by an employee within the scope of his or her employment."

The appeals court looked at the sculptor's status as an independent contractor under the subsection of the "work made for hire" definition, since sculpture is not one of the nine defined categories of works and the parties had not agreed in writing that the sculpture would be a work for hire.

On further appeal, the Supreme Court decided that general common law agency principles must be first applied to determine whether the work was prepared by an employee or an independent contractor. Depending upon the outcome of that determination, the employee—clause (1)—or independent contractor—clause (2)—subsection in Section 101 is to be applied.

Although the act does not define employee, employment, or related terms, the Court took the position that Congress meant them in their settled, common-law sense. Moreover, according to the Supreme Court, the general common law of agency must be relied on, rather than the law of any particular state, since the act is expressly intended to create a federal law of uniform, nationwide application.

In this case, the Supreme Court found the sculpture in question not to be a "work for hire," since the sculptor was an independent contractor, rather than an employee. Although CCNV directed enough of the work to ensure that the artist's work met their specifications, all other facts weighed heavily against finding an employment relationship.

On another issue, the Court did not decide whether CCNV is a joint author of the sculpture and, thus, a co-owner of the copyright. The federal district court was directed to determine if the parties prepared the work with the intention that their contributions be merged into inseparable or interdependent parts of a unitary whole.[13]

---

13. *Source:* Newsletter prepared by the Law Offices of Fenwick, Davis & West, Palo Alto, CA.

Note: *Firms or individuals engaged in research and development, as well as artistic endeavors, should implement a carefully prepared written assignment agreement with both independent contractors and employees to avoid litigation over both the work for hire and co-ownership provisions of the Act. Such assignments should cover all types of intellectual property, not merely copyrightable works.*

A sample *Assignment of Copyright* can be found in Appendix I as Exhibit 9.

Your Turn

Please answer the following questions:

► What are the rights of the owner of a copyright?

► What three allegations are grounds for objection to an application for copyright?

1. _____

2. _____

3. _____

TRADEMARK RIGHTS

In this time of mass communication, trademarks are almost as significant a part of a product's identification as what the product does. Certain well-known trademarks have tremendous value on their own. This has led, on occasion, to cross-licensing of marks; names like Coke, Radio Shack, Xerox and Pepsi automatically trigger identification with goods or services.

If your business has or will have a distinctive name or mark for its goods and services, you may want to protect it as you would patent an invention or copyright an operating manual.

Trademarks can be protected by either state or federal law, or both. Even under the so-called common law, a trademark could be protected if it could be shown to the court that someone else was improperly using the mark that you had already established.

Registration of the mark under law automatically establishes the notice of your claim in the mark and preempts some of the difficulties involved in establishing a trademark infringement or improper use case at common law.

Let's look first at what constitutes a protectable mark or name.

A Protectable Mark

▶ *The mark, symbol or name must be unique and not used by anyone else in the same class of goods or services.* This is quite a challenge, since so many names, marks and symbols are already in use. Advertising agencies and other creative resources can help a business find a unique mark, symbol or name.

▶ *The mark cannot be an unmodified generic noun or phrase.* *Bill's Place* could become a tradename, but *Place* could not.

▶ *The mark must be used in commerce.* To justify your claim to exclusive use, you must show that you are using it. If you are applying for federal protection, you must be using it in interstate commerce; you need to send a product or item containing the mark interstate, with proof of the shipment.

If you have developed a distinctive mark, logo, design or other device to identify a product or service with you, it must be so used. This means that a wonderfully designed logo for the product that you plan to bring out next year cannot receive trademark protection until it is, in fact, used.

This does not mean that there is no protection until you are ready to use a mark. You have at least a common law copyright on the writing. Also, the law allows some time for bringing the product or service to market. In fact, the revised Trademark Act of 1988 even lets you apply for trademark registration prior to use as long as you confirm your intention to use the mark in commerce.

► *Use of the mark must be continuous.* This means that the mark cannot be used and then abandoned, with an expectation that your exclusive rights will continue.

Do You Have to Register Your Mark?

The answer is *no*. Like the automatic protection afforded copyrights when the material is created, a trademark can become proprietary merely by using it in connection with a product or service.

If you can prove that a trademark is yours, the courts will usually stop someone else from using it and may even award damages for the other's misuse. Some people use the initials ™ to indicate their claim of a trademark, or ℠ for servicemark protection. These can be done without any legal proceedings. Before using a mark or name, be certain that you are not infringing someone else's mark.

Registration of the mark at the Patent and Trademark Office is recommended for certain practical reasons. Among the advantages of registration are the notice given through the *PTO Official Gazette* to all others of your claim in the mark. It also allows you to use the ® mark in connection with the name; this acts as a warning to others not to infringe your rights in the mark.

Since many more people and firms register marks than use them, the Trademark Act of 1988 lowered the protection period for a mark from 20 years to 10 years. As long as you use your mark, you may seek protection for an initial period of 10 years and subsequent renewal periods of 10 years.

Note: The distinction between trademarks and servicemarks is often confusing.

► A trademark is associated with a product.

► A servicemark is associated with service.

For example, my firm, Mediate-Tech, Inc., uses the servicemark *MTI Mediation* to describe our mediation process; we use the trademark *MTI Press* to identify the printed and audio tapes we offer.

Should You Choose State or Federal Protection?

To answer this question, you must decide where your business using the mark will operate. If you expect to operate primarily within one state, you may not need federal protection. If you expect your business that uses the mark to operate in several states or interstate—between and among various states—federal protection is best for you.

Consider these factors when you are deciding where to seek protection.

▶ The federal trademark registration requirements are far broader than any state protection—presumably making it easier to find a registerable mark

▶ Notice to others under federal law is national and not restricted to one state, territory or region. Some foreign countries allow virtually automatic registration if the applicant already has a U.S. registered mark.

▶ Legal relief under federal law is better than most states, although some states have tougher penalties for infringement.

▶ With federal protection, it is possible to seek exclusion of foreign infringing goods from entry into the United States.

▶ Entry to federal courts for judicial relief is automatic. It may be possible to go to federal court if you have a state or even common law mark, but there must be federal jurisdiction established on some basis other than federal trademark protection.

Now that we have discussed the advantages of the federal law, let's take a look at the Trademark Act of 1946—the Lanham Act. This continues to be a good law, although it has been amended recently. The Act provides for two registers of marks at the federal level:

1. The Principal Register

2. The Supplemental Register

The Principal Register is where the original and distinctive marks are registered. Marks not registerable there may be registerable in the Supplemental Register if they "are capable of distinguishing the applicant's goods and have been used in commerce for at least one year."

Goods registered in the Principal Register provide the following trademark protection benefits.

1. Constructive notice to the nation of registrant's claim of ownership

2. Prima facie evidence of validity and right to use the mark in accordance with limitations, if any, stated in the registration

3. Right to prevent importation into the United States for infringing goods—that is, bearing a mark already registered in the United States

The three protections listed above are not granted under the Supplemental Register. However, registrants:

▶ Can sue in federal courts

▶ May be able to register their marks in foreign countries that require home country registration first

▶ Can prevent registration of the mark by another in either register

Names and marks that have been registered are listed in the *Official Gazette* of the PTO.

Obtaining Trademark Protection

Common law protection arises out of the legal use of the mark without formalized registration. Consult individual state trademark registration statutes for state procedures regarding protection. Here, we will look principally at federal protection.

Registration under the Act requires that the mark meet all the standards outlined above. Registration is by application on appropriate forms to the PTO. Printed forms are available from the PTO for individuals, firms, corporations and associations. Drawings of the proposed mark must accompany the application.

Since so many applications are filed and so many names and marks are similar, it is advisable to have a trademark search conducted prior to going to the expense and trouble of formal filing; this will give you a reasonably good idea that your name or mark is available.

Patent and trademark attorneys can conduct these searches. Private firms and organizations also conduct searches at the federal and/or state level. If you need a federal or state search and do not know how to find someone to do it, contact a patent attorney or look in the Washington, D.C. telephone directory.

Trademarks can represent a substantial asset to companies. For example, I was told during a trip to Israel that MacDonalds went to court in Israel to stop a firm from using the name "MacDavids" with a logo that contained arches in the background. The interesting twist is that MacDonalds was not even operating in Israel at that time; they apparently believed that people could be influenced by the usurpation—in their view—of their distinctive combination of name and mark. MacDavids continues to serve hamburgers in Israel, but their logo is a caricature of Uncle Sam.

Your Turn

Please answer the following questions:

▶ List three examples of a protectable mark or name.

1. _____

2. _____

3. _____

▶ Is it necessary to go through legal proceedings to get a trademark?

▶ What is the period of protection for a trademark?

▶ Is it necessary to obtain federal protection for a trademark? State protection?

► List four advantages of federal trademark protection.

1. _____

2. _____

3. _____

4. _____

► Who, in your locality, can do a trademark search?

These guidelines will help you use a trademark properly.

TRADEMARK GUIDELINES

1. Use the mark, as an adjective only, for the generic name of your product—e.g., Laura Little Art Pencils.

2. Be certain that when you use the mark, you signify the mark as distinguished from other words—e.g., "When you need to make a sketch that truly reflects your talent, be sure to use only *Laura Little Art Pencils.*"

3. Be consistent and uniform each time you use the mark.

TRADE SECRET PROTECTION

As described above, most of the mechanisms to preserve a property interest in some intellectual property of your firm involve disclosure of the details of the item to a governmental agency.

Suppose you feel a product or process is confidential and proprietary and you would rather not disclose how it is made. Can you protect it?

The answer is *yes,* if the information can be kept secret. The formula for Coca-Cola and the recipe for Kentucky Fried Chicken have never been patented, presumably because such legal action would involve disclosing what the suppliers see as secret information.

Material that is considered a business trade secret must meet certain general requirements. It must:

- ▶ Be considered as giving the firm some type of competitive advantage
- ▶ Be treated by management as confidential information
- ▶ Be information that is not generally known outside the firm

This kind of protection is generally obtained by contract. You preserve your secrecy by having employees and others sign a confidentiality agreement stating they will keep your information private and confidential.

A sample Confidentiality Agreement can be found in Appendix I as Exhibit 10.

To obtain court assistance in preserving company confidential or trade secret information, you must be able to show the court that you have taken every reasonable step possible to keep the information private and confidential.

The following checklist will help you keep your confidential information preserved for your firm's own use only.

BUSINESS CONFIDENTIALITY CHECKLIST

- ▶ Have we prepared confidentiality or nondisclosure agreements?
- ▶ Are all employees who need confidential information required to sign?
- ▶ Are outsiders who have access to confidential information required to sign a nondisclosure form?
- ▶ Is information that is to be considered confidential marked and clearly delineated as such?
- ▶ Is confidential information treated as such inside the firm?
- ▶ Have we taken reasonable steps to restrict access to confidential information?
- ▶ Do we have—or do we need—a policy regarding confidentiality and secrecy of certain information?

You also want to avoid being accused of taking someone else's information. The best way of doing so is by being clear and careful about the information you receive from outsiders. Most firms will not even accept ideas submitted by outsiders without a signed waiver of some type or limitation to the submitter to rights under the patent laws.

Trade secret protection is both easy and difficult.

► It is easy in that no formal, outside filing, forms or registration with any state agency or any entity outside your own organization is required.

► It is difficult in that to establish that someone else violated your rights, you must show that the information meets all the requirements outlined above and that you did your best to restrict access.

It is up to you to decide what products, goods, information, names, marks, logos and data is of value to you and to your business. Once you are clear on this decision, you must decide what you will do to preserve these valuable property rights.

ASK YOURSELF

▶ Identify the distinctive and distinguishing trademarks, logos and names that apply to your products and services that you would want to register.

▶ Discuss whether it would be appropriate to add the proprietary claiming initials ™ and/or ℠ to your products/services.

▶ Describe the procedure to register a trademark within your state.

▶ Assess your firm's information to identify the information or company data that should be treated as confidential. Include the steps that you have taken to preserve the confidentiality of such information.

▶ Explain your procedures to protect confidentiality of information with regard to both employees and outsiders.

BUSINESS TROUBLE

YOU HAVE OPTIONS

When trouble occurs within your organization or poses a threat from the outside, you have options you may not be aware of. Most people immediately conclude that they must run to counsel and seek their rights under the law. While this certainly may be true under a variety of situations, it may not be true of *all* situations.

If you can, the first thing to do when you find your business in trouble is to try to resolve the problem yourself.[14]

THE TRADITIONAL LEGAL PROCESS

Traditional legal responses to conflict in a business are divided into two general categories. Lawyers refer to these as:

▶ Remedies at law

▶ Remedies in equity

The difference between law and equity is purely academic in modern legal times; it was relevant in older Anglo-Saxon legal systems when judges needed power beyond awarding damages to an aggrieved party—as in the law. A separate system developed out of this need, which allowed for the doing of justice—equity—by the judge, who was called a chancellor when he sat in equity.

Equity allowed judges to issue injunctions that prohibited certain conduct and forced parties to do what they were supposed to do. When money damages alone were not sufficient to "do justice," the court had the equitable power to take alternative action.

---

14. See also *Ironing It Out: Seven Simple Steps to Resolving Conflict* by Charles P. Lickson, J.D., available from MTI Press at 1-800-967-4555 and *Managing Disagreement Constructively* by Herbert S. Kindler, Ph.D., Crisp Publications.

Today, in most jurisdictions, the distinctions between the law judge and the equity chancellor are symbolic, if they exist at all; however, the ancient remedies are still relevant because they dictate what the court has the power to do, to correct the wrong or compensate the aggrieved party.

Where someone has suffered damage, either through a breach of contract or because of the negligence or intentional act of another, money damages can be awarded to compensate them fairly. Damages in contract breaches are measured by placing the victim in the financial position he or she would have been in had the agreement not been breached.

In noncontractual wrongs such as negligence, the measure of damages is the sum that fairly compensates the victim by repaying the special damages—for example, medical bills and lost wages—plus additional damages as the judge or jury sees fit to cover the pain and suffering or intangible loss.

Money damages are not always sufficient to do justice. For example, imagine that the owner of an art gallery sold a reproduction of a painting to a customer, but inadvertently delivered the original. When the gallery owner asked for the painting back and offered either to refund the money or give the customer the reproduction, the customer refused. Money damages would not be sufficient because the painting is unique. The gallery owner would need to go to court to seek an order that would force the customer to return the painting.

If a substantial injustice would be done by letting the customer keep the painting or if the gallery owner could show the court that there was no adequate remedy at law, the gallery owner could appeal to the *equity side* of the court for special remedies. These remedies include injunctions and actions to prevent unjust enrichment. Following that rationale, it is probable that the court would order the customer to return the original painting.

Using the many and varied capabilities of the legal system usually requires a lawyer and can be very costly as well as slow. It can also be very disruptive to a business. If the trouble manifests itself as a dispute between the employer and an employee, between an outsider and an employee or between two employees, the best solution may be to seek a resolution without involving the framework of the organized legal system.

You can always seek redress within the legal system by consulting counsel or even going to court yourself. Under general principles of constitutional law and the American justice system, most courts allow parties to represent themselves. Appearances by individuals without counsel are referred to in law as either *in propria person* or as *pro se* appearances.

This holdover from earlier, more simple times in our history still prevails in small claims courts and in full trial courts in most states. Where corporations are involved, some jurisdictions have limitations on people representing themselves—since, in the eyes of the law, the corporation itself is an individual and, as such, cannot be represented in court by a nonattorney.

What if you do not want to go to court?

Alternatives are available, as you will see in this case study of a problem that arose for one small, private accounting firm. Notice how the dispute resolution possibilities work out.

CASE STUDY

Joe's Special Assignment

The president of the accounting firm's largest client notified Jim's boss that he is very unhappy with the job Jim did on a special assignment to develop a new financial package for their firm.

The client claimed that the system did not work. The client further alleged that the system would never work because of errors in judgment and execution of the work Jim designed and managed. In addition, the client alleged that Jim violated confidentiality by releasing client data to a subcontractor without first obtaining permission.

Jim had a history of producing good work and his clients trusted him. In fact, he had worked on this account for more than five years. In all that time, there never was even a question about Jim's loyalty, ability to serve as the client's software systems consultant or the trust inherent in Jim's access to the client's most sensitive data.

This nightmare scenario may sound like fiction, but in this era of elevated professional liability and exploding litigation, it must be taken most seriously.

Does Jim need his own lawyer in this situation? Will his own firm defend him? What kind of future can he hope for with the firm? What are the financial and ethical considerations of these allegations?

In fact, the accounting firm received an letter from the client's attorney threatening suit if the systems problems were not corrected and substantial damages were not paid for the alleged breach of fiduciary trust relationship. The letter threatened the firm and the individual partners; it named Jim specifically as a potential lawsuit target.

What are the firm's and Jim's options?

Assuming that his consulting or retainer agreement did not contain any special language, the accounting firm could proceed to litigation or choose to negotiate. The choice would be theirs.

Let's assume they were to demand a settlement that is well beyond what Jim's errors and omissions insurance carrier is willing to pay. Jim and the firm would reject the demand and the lawsuit papers would be served. Perhaps the local newspaper would delight in the story and other clients might look at Jim in questioning ways. A new client whom

Jim had been after for months might advise Jim that another consultant had been chosen.

If Jim's firm retains counsel through his malpractice policy, they would advise Jim that he should expect a deluge of paperwork for discovery, and estimates of the cost of defending the case would probably indicate that the firm would not make a profit that year. Not only would this mean elimination of any firm bonuses, but it could even affect the amount of his draw.

Jim would wonder how his partners felt about all this and how he would get his work done while he responds to the needs and pressures of this case. In fact, Jim would even wonder whether he should continue with his firm. Let's face it, after all the dust settles, his future at the firm would not be rosy.

Would it have to go this way?

If his contract had special language or Jim could persuade the other side to consider it, Alternative Dispute Resolution (ADR) would provide an alternative. With an ADR clause in the consulting or retainer agreement, the parties must use mediation or other agreed process to see if they can resolve their differences *before* formal accusations are made or legal process begins.

ADR is often the perfect medium for liability and potential settlement issues. A closer look at ADR is well worth considering for business people at all levels, service providers and other professionals in their working relationships.

ALTERNATE DISPUTE RESOLUTION

Almost everyone, including those in the legal profession, agrees that traditional litigation may not be able to handle all of the civil cases pending in our courts these days. Not only is traditional litigation expensive, it usually also involves serious delays; while parties and counsel prepare for court, waiting for court dates can have a tremendous impact on usual work.

Ask any colleague who has been involved in commercial litigation and they will tell you—as Jim would in this scenario—it is virtually impossible to accomplish anything else while a big case is being prepared.

Recently, ADR has been receiving increased press and raising more interest among lawyers and potential parties. This is especially true since access to the civil side of traditional courts may be limited—if not eliminated—in the near future by dockets crowded or even overwhelmed by criminal cases.

Business Week magazine has reported that transaction costs and damage awards are having a tremendously adverse effect on America's business economy. At a recent conference in New York it was reported that U.S. corporations currently spend over $80 billion in legal fees, mostly related to litigation. In response to these outrageous legal fees, over 500 U.S. corporations have signed a pledge to use ADR wherever possible; many U.S. law firms are—perhaps reluctantly—also getting aboard.

What can be done when you cannot get to court or choose an alternative approach?

A number of organizations both within and outside of the judicial system have come up with alternative processes to the traditional litigation, aimed especially at commercial cases of the type involving Jim's firm. These organizations range from quasi-public entities such as court mediation groups to private for-profit firms.

How Does ADR Work?

Most of the organizations or firms that offer ADR services work in somewhat the same way. The process is simple. One or more parties decide directly or through their attorneys to submit the issue to the private resolution system. A filing fee, which includes staff review of the issue and a recommendation on the best ADR method for handling the problem, is sometimes paid.

While it may not represent the unanimous opinion of all practitioners, ADR is generally thought to include arbitration as well as mediation and conciliation.

Arbitration

Arbitration is a proceeding whereby a neutral individual or group of individuals, known as a panel, hear attorneys and/or parties describe their case; both sides present evidence and the panel makes a decision. The finding in arbitration can be binding or not, depending on the prior agreement of the parties.

Arbitration is a private process not involving the government court system—although binding arbitration decisions can be made judgments of the court.

Many commercial agreements, especially in construction and securities transactions, use arbitration as the exclusive means of resolution. The Supreme Court of the United States has upheld these clauses as binding.

Your Turn

Please answer the following questions:

▶ Name two legal responses to trouble in business.

- _____

- _____

▶ What are the advantages of ADR?

- _____

- _____

- _____

Mediation and Conciliation

Mediation is the agreement by two or more parties to allow a neutral third party—a mediator—to assist them in reaching their own resolution of the problem. If they wish, the mediation is held in the presence of the parties and their counsel. With the assistance of the mediator, all have an opportunity to define the problem and work toward a resolution.

Conciliation is similar to mediation; it involves the agreement of the parties to enroll the assistance of a neutral third party to assist them in resolving their own dispute.

The major difference between mediation and conciliation is that in mediation all parties remain present, whereas in conciliation the neutral third party meets with each party individually and acts as a conduit or communications resource and facilitator.

In conciliation, the parties are usually not in each other's presence. Conciliation is often used for long distance resolution—for example, by phone—and/or shuttle diplomacy, such as in the sensitive Middle East negotiations.

Mediation is often the method of choice. It offers a powerful conflict resolution method where confidentiality is preserved, quick resolution is possible and expenses can be controlled.

Another major attraction of mediation in the commercial or professional context is the measure of control the disputant has over the process. While mediators can make major contributions to the process of agreement, if the process is to succeed, the parties themselves must finally reach an accord.

More than 80% of all cases submitted to mediation result in an agreed resolution. The theory behind this success is quite simple: If more than 99% of all civil cases settle before trial anyway, why not try to settle early by using a neutral mediator?

Mediation has proven effective as the method of choice for resolution where there has been, or continues to be, a relationship between the parties in the dispute. While mediation of ordinary commercial cases is relatively new, the process has been used successfully for years in labor disputes and in divorce and family cases.

A special challenge to resolution arises where there are complex and difficult factors, such as special business or fiduciary relationships—as in Jim's case. Litigation is often prolonged because of the complex and legally technical issues that can easily confuse both judge and jurors.

Sometimes, even counsel has trouble synthesizing the issues into an easy form for a judge or jury to understand; and, all too often, counsel does not even understand the issues. Also, with delays, litigation can end up costing more than the disputed issue is worth, or it may take so long that a company or professional firm goes out of business because of its inability to get timely resolution.

Both businesspeople and company counsel are finding an increasing interest and acceptance of mediation as a low-risk method to resolve disputes. The sample clauses in Exhibit 11 in Appendix I can be inserted into any agreements where parties are willing to look at possibilities for resolving disputes in a low cost, low impact manner.

In Jim's case, mediation seems to provide a perfect forum for the clarification and appropriate resolution of the client complaints, without the embarrassment, delays and costs of traditional litigation. In mediation, any party can be represented by counsel or appear pro se; no one need agree to anything that is not in their best interests.

The United States remains a lawyer-based society. In fact, America has been called the most litigious society in the world. In other countries, such as Japan, it is considered far less desirable to go to court than to settle a dispute oneself. In Africa and China, elders or community leaders assist parties to resolve conflicts; courts are available as a last, and very undesirable, choice.

Many cases are not appropriate for alternative dispute resolution. Sometimes legal judgments are desirable or necessary. But before aggrieved parties rush to call their attorneys, they might consider using a neutral mediator or conciliator to assist them in resolving the matter.

After all, who knows best about your issue and your business—the parties or the attorneys?

ASK YOURSELF

► Explain the reasons why many business-related problems are best solved by the persons most involved.

► How open are you to working out problems before they degenerate into legal issues?

► Discuss the degree to which your agreements lend themselves to mediation clauses.

► How willing is your attorney to consider ADR when resolving disputes?

OTHER LEGAL CONSIDERATIONS

"GREEN" ISSUES AND BUSINESS

Several other supplementary areas are of interest in business law. This chapter provides a starting point for further research.

These days, no one has to tell you twice that considerations about the environment are relevant to both business and private life. This chapter outlines the environmental factors that businesses need to consider.

Most environmental regulation is relatively new. As anyone over the age of adolescence knows, there was a time when the environment was just there. People who cared about it were the *hippies* and *greenies*—or whatever the activists were called at any moment. Many of us were concerned about the environment in our own way. Perhaps we did not leave garbage at our picnic site, or we may have used ecologically sound detergent for our laundry; whatever form it took, our commitment was usually limited and purely voluntary.

Some people may look with melancholy at the days when, both in our business and in our private lives, we were left to deal with the environment in your individual ways—if at all. Today, the days of carefree business practices are behind us. Whether we like it or not, a new era of public concern and legislative regulation about certain environmental issues is upon us.

Environmental law is emerging rapidly as a major specialty in law practice. This chapter discusses the general considerations about environmental laws and rules that apply to any business or profession. It will not include those environmentally sensitive fields of business in which the statutes, rules and regulations are so complex that it takes a legal specialist to make virtually every decision.

The statutory basis for environmental regulation derives from the legal premise that the government is the ultimate guardian of the air, water, air waves and open lands. As conservator of these resources, the government has the inherent power to determine appropriate conduct and usage of these public assets.

If your business uses or affects these resources, you should understand the laws and regulations that cover them. Generally speaking, these laws include:

- ▶ Land Use
- ▶ Natural resources
- ▶ Wetlands—saltwater
- ▶ Lakes and rivers—pertaining to water rights, flood control and natural preservation
- ▶ Mining and mineral rights
- ▶ Oil and gas law
- ▶ Environmental Protection Acts—federal and state
- ▶ Drought and water usage regulations
- ▶ Storage and disposal rules and regulations for certain substances
- ▶ Fertilizer and pesticide control regulations
- ▶ Clean-up statutes—these are usually applied retroactively
- ▶ Clean air, water and land statutes
- ▶ Soil conservation laws
- ▶ Natural places restoration or preservation laws

Remember that this list is by no means complete. Moreover, many of the regulations have stiff penalties and carry what lawyers call *joint and several liability*—which means that all parties are liable for the damage, both as a group and individually—and can close down your business for noncompliance.

To find out more about what regulations govern your business, you can get help from:

- ▶ Your state or city health department

- ▶ Your state's department of environmental protection

- ▶ The zoning and planning commission

- ▶ Someone in the environmental law area of a local university or law school

- ▶ Regional offices of the federal Environmental Protection Agency

Find out about your business's environmental needs and requirements before someone comes after you. It better for the environment you live in, and it is a lot less expensive to comply in advance than to defend yourself and to comply by retrofit.

INSURANCE AND RISK MANAGEMENT

Insurance minimizes financial risk in the event of certain things happening that could adversely affect your business. If you are in business, you ought to be insured.

As a matter of law, you may be required to carry some type of insurance. For example:

- ▶ If you have employees, you must carry workers' compensation insurance and unemployment insurance.

- ▶ You may be required to carry health or hospitalization insurance.

- ▶ Surety bonds and liability policies are other insurance products that may be required by law.

► If you use a motor vehicle in your business, you are required to carry appropriate insurance.

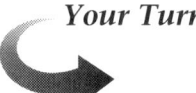

Your Turn

Please answer the following questions:

► What insurance are you required to have?

► Is it enough?

There is no magic formula to know if you have enough insurance; you will need to analyze your business needs and ability to pay. While an insurance professional will be happy to advise you, beware of hard sell or prepackaged business insurance policies, which may not be appropriate for you.

An insurance policy is a contract. Thus, everything you have already learned about contracts applies to your insurance policy negotiations and the policies you choose.

These kinds of contracts have several nuances. First, insurance is regulated in every state. State laws deal with things such as premium determination factors, determining classes of risk and requirements of licensure for agents or brokers. Some states even regulate the language and the form of insurance contracts offered for sale within their state.

Insurance gives you the opportunity to establish a plan to minimize the risk of your business. For a fee, the insurance company absorbs some of the financial risk.

To create a risk plan, you should:

► List all the potential risks you can imagine that could affect you business.

► Note which risks carry financial exposure and which risks carry other kinds of exposure.

► As to the financial risks, see if you are able to find an insurance policy that helps pay for exposure if the need arises.

Keep the following general points in mind when you make your insurance policy purchase decision.

► Higher deductibles mean lower premiums.

► Taking certain safety and well being action can lower premiums—for example, installing fire doors and sprinklers.

► Watch carefully for the exclusions. Make certain that the risks you need covered are not excluded from the policy.

► Are there some risks that you are willing to self-insure— that you would be willing to pay out of the business's own funds in the event of loss?

► Differentiate risks that would be devastating from those that your business could tolerate.

► Factor in your ability to pay the premiums on an annual basis—or other basis of commitment for the policy.

► Identify any risks that are unique and that you may be able to satisfy with individual, one-time policies or surety bonds.

As a contract, the insurance policy requires the contracting elements:

► Offer

► Acceptance

► Consideration

► Legal purpose

► Capacity to make a contract

In the insurance context, these legal elements may take on special attributes. For example, with insurance policies, the application is your offer. It is accepted or not at the home office, and it is not a contract until it is accepted. Be aware that the insurance agent is usually not legally empowered—under the laws of agency—to bind the insurance company; he or she may be permitted to issue a binder—temporary coverage.

All information required by the insurance application must be carefully and accurately filled in. A misrepresentation—something that is untrue and you know it is untrue—is grounds for the insurance company to revoke the policy and even refuse to pay benefits, even though you have paid all premiums.

Sometimes insurers will require you to have an insurable interest in the protected person or goods of the insurance. This is a requirement of public policy to prevent people from insuring anyone or anything with which they do not have a genuine contact or interest.

For example, to protect the firm in the event of her untimely death, The Laura Little Group, Inc. might want to obtain "key person" life insurance on Laura's life. Certainly, the firm would have an insurable interest in Laura. However, an acquaintance of Laura's from her Rotary club meetings could not take out insurance on Laura's life; such a policy would violate public policy and would be void.

Your business might need or be required to have several policies in addition to the state-administered insurance programs, such as workers' compensation and unemployment insurance (over which you have little control or discretion if you have employees).

Some examples are:

- ▶ Fire insurance protects your business from loss from fire. Insurers limit their liability to pay only for what they call hostile fires—fires that are unintentionally started.

- Auto insurance usually covers liability—claims by third persons—and collision covers damage to the insured vehicle.

- Business interruption insurance covers losses to business revenue if the business cannot function due to a covered event, such as fire or earthquake.

- Life insurance assists the business in obtaining replacement talent if a key employee dies.

- Health and disability insurance protects against the costs of hospitalization, certain healthcare costs and inability of an employee to work over a long period of time.

- Errors and omissions protects professionals such as doctors, lawyers, accountants and others from exposure due to claims of negligence or oversight. To be licensed in some states, certain professionals, such as lawyers, must maintain active errors and omissions policies.

You can see that insurance can minimize exposure in the unforeseen or unpleasant event of certain losses. You may want to consult a qualified business insurance specialist about what is best for your business.

Your Turn

Please answer the following questions:

- Does your business activity require insurance under state law or licensure?

- Do your property, business activity and key personnel require insurance coverage?

- What is the best insurance for your business risks?

FRANCHISING—A SPECIAL LEGAL CHALLENGE

Franchises have been defined as rights to engage in a business developed by someone else. As anyone contemplating a franchise business knows, the key element in such an undertaking is the opportunity to participate in a packaged business.

Franchises have the potential for a win-win outcome, because the person obtaining the rights (the franchisee) learns from the franchiser (the originator of the concept) and begins a readily identifiable and presumably attractive service or product undertaking. The franchiser shares in the revenue and, in exchange, is usually required to assist in the franchisee's success.

Franchises allow the franchiser to expand without the capital needed to finance each operation. Franchises can also add substantial revenue to the franchisers' coffers. The franchisee has the opportunity—for which he or she has paid—to benefit from the coattails of a successful business and to participate in a larger network than they could probably do on their own.

Franchises fall into two categories:

▶ Package or product franchises

▶ Business opportunity venture franchising

If you already are involved in a franchise or seriously contemplating such an operation, make sure you are working with a lawyer knowledgeable in franchise law. This section addresses some of the legal considerations about franchising.

All the requirements of contract law apply to a franchise, since a franchise is a contract to participate in someone else's business. As a result of some past misconduct in the sale of franchise rights, there has been some regulation enacted at both the state and the federal levels.

The U.S. Federal Trade Commission (FTC) prohibits misleading advertising and claims. So do consumer protection and justice agencies of many states. The FTC makes the following recommendations to anyone who is considering entrance into franchise agreements.

▶ Study all documents, especially the contract, before signing.

▶ Consult a lawyer before making a binding commitment.

► Be certain that oral promises appear in writing in the franchise agreement.

► Talk to others who have been involved with the franchise to assess their experience. Make sure you are talking to people who have put their own money up and not representatives brought in by the franchiser.

► Before relying on the earnings of other franchisees to determine what you might expect to earn, check the financial statement carefully and find out the basis and method of earnings for the others. When you assess the earning ability of the operation, do not forget to consider the costs of doing business and what buyers had to pay the franchiser.

The Franchise Disclosure Rule, enforced by the FTC, requires potential franchisees to receive detailed franchise information; franchise candidates must receive written disclosure documents at least 10 days before signing contracts. Disclosure statements are required to contain some 20 categories of information, including such items as:

► Business, legal and financial history of the principal players of the franchiser

► Details of operating expenses for the franchise

► How many franchises have been sold and the failure rate

► Information on how to end, cancel or renew the franchise agreement

All of the information in the disclosure statement must be based upon sound business and accounting principles.

Several states have enacted laws to protect citizens from unscrupulous franchise offers. These laws vary but usually include:

► Some provision requiring registration of franchisers or salespeople before offers can be made or accepted

► Escrow or bonding for franchise fees

▶ Full disclosure of all information—states must meet or exceed the FTC requirements

▶ Specific wording in the contract covering termination, cancellation, renewal and return of funds, if any

A Franchising Checklist

If you are seriously contemplating a franchise arrangement, the following checklist will help you determine what is fair and appropriate for yourself.

▶ Do I know the franchiser, or have I checked it out with such groups as the Better Business Bureau?

▶ How long has the franchiser been in business? How well has it done in the past?

▶ What, if anything, do I know or what can I learn about the operating principals of the franchiser, including reputation and past successes or failures?

▶ Do I understand the company's financial statements? Can I tell where and how the company derives most revenue?

▶ How does the company choose its franchisees—is it more than you pay your money and you are in?

▶ Where will I operate? If it is an exclusive territory, is it adequately defined?

▶ How well can I expect to be supported by the franchiser? At what cost?

▶ Is the franchise agreement fair, or is it slanted in favor of franchiser?

▶ Do I fully understand the extent of my financial commitment—including franchise rights fee, operating capital and other needs?

▶ Have I contacted experienced franchise counsel to assist me in negotiating and executing the agreement when I am ready?

Franchises can be a wonderful way to obtain an instant business. They are also fraught with danger. Be certain your eyes are open before you go forward in this direction.[15]

If you are going to be involved with a franchise, the first thing you need to do is to find someone who is a franchisee—not necessarily of the one you contemplate, although that would be best. Discuss both the good news and bad news about being a franchisee. Contact the agency in your state that polices franchise offers. Ask them for any information they have about buying franchise rights. And, be certain your franchise project is registered.

INTERNATIONAL BUSINESS OPPORTUNITIES

In this day of speedy data communications and fast jet travel, international business is no longer unique; in fact, it is becoming the norm as increasing numbers of U.S. companies are finding markets for their goods and services outside the borders of the U.S. Activities may involve short-length transactions with Canada or long distance undertakings with Singapore. One thing is clear: U.S. business is no longer doing business in the U.S. alone.

If you will be exporting or importing, there may be federal regulations that apply to the United States end of the transactions. These include:

► Customs duties

► Tariffs—regarding some goods

► Restrictions on certain items or with certain places considered unfriendly to the United States

The Commerce Department's Bureau of International Commerce will help familiarize you with regulations and requirements that apply to your business and how to

---

15. See also *Buying Your First Franchise* by Rebecca Luhn, Ph.D., Crisp Publications, 1993.

comply. You can also contact U.S. Customs regarding customs duties and the State Department regarding what goods or services can be shipped where without violating U.S. law.

Remember that the other country may have it own regulations. Contact the economic attache or development officer from the embassy or consulate of the nation with which you expect to do business.

Your state may have an economic development office or other office created to promote expansion of trade. These people can be exceptionally helpful regarding complying with state and federal regulatory requirements. If they know you are interested in exporting goods or services that could benefit the state's economy, they may even help you make some good business contacts.

Commercial transactions are relevant to any discussion of international business. Most financial transactions that pertain to international business are handled through negotiable instruments or electronic transfers. These exchanges, known as EDI or electronic data interchange, are invaluable to long distance business transactions both in the United States and the international domain. Today, for example, EDI is commonplace among banks and major businesses.

Speaking of banks, you cannot successfully undertake international business without a good banking relationship. Be certain your bank has an EDI capability with corresponding banks in the country where you will be doing business. Make sure that you also have a friend at the bank whom you can talk to and who understands the needs and requirements of international transactions.

One major area of concern about international business arrangements is what to do if something goes wrong. After all, it is not like bringing suit in the next town or even the neighboring state. Many firms add an international arbitration clause to their working agreements. I prefer a mediation clause, followed by arbitration if mediation is not successful.

International business can be exciting as well as rewarding. Whenever you are contracting in an international context, be certain that your attorney is experienced in international transactions. A number of U.S. and non-U.S. law firms now have offices in major foreign locations, as well as in U.S. cities. While this is not an automatic guarantee that they will know what they are doing, it does indicate the firm's commitment to international practice and to being knowledgeable about both U.S. law and the laws of their offices abroad.[16]

---

16. See also *Winning in Foreign Markets* by Michele D. Forzley, Crisp Publications, 1994.

ASK YOURSELF

▶ What assistance and insights into the legal requirements and practical considerations will you want to gain from the consulate of the country where you will be doing business, or from the economic, development or business attache in their embassy in Washington, D.C.?

▶ What assistance will you seek from the international commerce office at your nearest Commerce Department regional office or the Bureau of International Commerce in Washington, D.C., for assistance in doing business with the particular country?

APPENDIX I
SAMPLE FORMS

It's not the form but the substance that counts.

—Old Saying

Having the right form helps.

—New Saying

EXHIBIT 1

Certificate of Doing Business

TOWN CLERK'S OFFICE

SMALLVILLE, ST 00011

Please take notice that Laura Anne Little of Smallville is conducting an unincorporated business known as "Laura Little Studio" located at 410 Maple Avenue, Smallville, ST 00011.

Dated at Smallville, this _____ day of_____, 1994.

Laura A. Little

Local business License No: _____

Note: These forms vary from jurisdiction to jurisdiction. Check with your city or county clerk or clerk of court to learn how to obtain a local certificate to do business and business license, if required by law.

EXHIBIT 2

Simple Partnership Agreement

AGREEMENT made as of this 14th day of March, 1993 between Laura A. Little of Smallville ("Laura") and Mary Contrari of Middletown ("Mary").

The parties intend to form a partnership to conduct an art studio and business on the following terms and conditions:

1. The partnership shall become effective upon the signing of this agreement and the paying in of $6,000 contribution by Laura and $4,000 by Mary.

2. The partnership shall be known as The Laura Little Studio.

3. The partnership will engage in the business of a full service art studio and advertising agency.

4. Business location will be 2774 Bedford Street, Smallville, ST 00011.

5. The partnership shall continue so long as both partners shall be alive. It may terminate sooner by agreement of the parties.

6. Profits and losses in the partnership shall be allocated 60% to Laura and 40% to Mary.

7. Partners shall draw a sum to be mutually agreed upon but not less than $200 per week.

8. Both partners shall devote full time and attention to the business of the partnership.

9. Laura shall be designated as the Managing Partner and shall have responsibility for the business and financial affairs of the partnership. Mary shall be designated the Creative Partner and have primary responsibility for creative efforts and marketing for the partnership.

10. At the dissolution of the partnership for any reason, the surplus, if any, shall be distributed 60% to Laura and 40% to Mary. The name and good will, if any, shall be sold with proceeds to be divided equally.

11. In the event of disagreement under this agreement or in running the affairs of the partnership, the partners agree to submit all unresolved issues to mediation prior to taking any legal action.

12. This agreement is the whole agreement of the parties with respect to the subject matter; it may not be amended except in writing; it may not be assigned by either party; and it shall be governed by the laws of State.

Signed at Smallville, ST.

_____

Laura Anne Little

_____

Mary Contrari

AFFIDAVIT

City of Smallville }

                 }   ss: State

County of Nether }

On this 14th day of March, 1993 came Laura A. Little and Mary Contrari, who each identified themselves to me and swore before me that their signatures on the foregoing document were their free act and deed.

_____

Dean O. Sauer

Notary Public No. 1009

(My commission expires 12-23-95)

EXHIBIT 3A

ARTICLES OF INCORPORATION
OF
THE LAURA LITTLE STUDIO, INC.

The undersigned, pursuant to Chapter 9 of Title 13.1 of the Code of Virginia, hereby executes the following articles of incorporation and sets forth the following:

1. The name of the corporation is: The Laura Little Studio, Inc.

2. The nature of the business and purposes to be transacted, promoted and carried on: are to engage in any lawful act or activity for which corporations may be organized under the General Corporation Laws of Virginia.

3. The total amount of the total authorized capital stock of this corporation is five thousand (5,000) shares of common stock of one cent ($.01) par value.

4. The post office address of the initial registered office is:

   100 East Main Street
   Smallville, VA 22000

   and the name of the initial registered agent at such address is Jon Smith who is a resident of Virginia and an officer and director of the corporation.

5. The names and addresses of the directors are:

   Jon Smith   160 Owens Road
                          Smallville, VA 22000

   Charles Armbruster   608 James Drive
                          Smallville, VA 22000

   Adolph Byrnes   10 East Maple Street
                          Smallville, VA 22000

6. The registered office is located in the City of Smallville.

INCORPORATOR:

_____

Jon Smith
Date: April 25, 1993

Note: Most states have a printed form for simple corporations.

EXHIBIT 3B

Cover Letter for Articles of Incorporation

JON SMITH

April 25, 1993

Office of the Clerk of the
State Corporation Commission
Post Office Box 1197
Capitol City, ST 00001

Re: Articles of Incorporation
     The Laura Little Studio, Inc.

Dear Sir or Madam:

Enclosed please find the Articles of Incorporation of the above named company and a check for $_____ covering the filing fee and the charter fee.

Please accept the enclosed Articles for filing and recording and return the Certificate of Incorporation to me at your earliest convenience.

Thank you for your assistance in this matter.

Sincerely,

Jon Smith

encls.

EXHIBIT 4

Joint Venture Agreement

AGREEMENT entered into as of _____ 19___, between The Laura Little Group, Inc. ("Group") and XYZ Designs ("Designs").

THE parties hereto desire to associate in a Joint Venture for the purpose of developing, manufacturing, importing and distributing an art studio management software program (the "Program").

IT IS AGREED AS FOLLOWS:

1. The Joint Venture shall be conducted in the following Phases:

(A) Phase One shall begin promptly upon the execution of this Agreement with the organization by the parties hereto of a corporation under the laws of _____ to be called *Art Programs, Inc.* (the "Company").

(B) Phase Two shall begin upon the conclusion of Phase One and shall continue until the Company shall have obtained its own facilities for developing, manufacturing and distributing the Programs.

(C) Phase Three shall begin upon the completion of the Company's own facilities for developing and manufacturing the Programs. During this phase the Company shall become fully operational in developing, manufacturing and distributing the Programs for its own account subject to the direction of the Company's Board of Directors.

2. The respective contributions of the parties to this joint venture shall be as follows:

(A) Group: $25,000 in initial capital of the Company to be paid in cash promptly upon the Company's formation. During Phase One, Group shall provide to the Company such support as is

(Exhibit 4 continued on next page)

EXHIBIT 4

(continued)

required by the Company under a discounted nonexclusive rate schedule attached hereto as Attachment A. At the completion of Phase Three, Company shall grant to the Group an exclusive distributorship to such Programs for the entire U.S. market.

(B) Designs: $25,000 in initial capital designated as follows: artwork of a reasonable value of $15,000 and $10,000 cash to be paid promptly upon formation. During all Phases, Designs shall offer reasonable support to Company in the area of art and design at reduced hourly rates.

3. At the end of each month, the parties shall submit to the Company an itemized list of expenses incurred, together with such substantiation as the Company may reasonably request, and at the beginning of Phase Three, the Company shall reimburse the parties for such expenses. In event the Company is not financially able to reimburse the parties, it shall execute its note to the parties payable within one year without interest.

4. The Company shall appropriately register or follow other formalities pursuant to U.S. and California law with regard to protecting the Programs in all respects and the names and marks associated therewith (and shall insure that it has fulfilled the requirements for foreign recognition where mutual pacts, treaties or conventions are in effect or come into effect with regard to selling the Programs outside the United States).

5. Neither party nor Company shall compete in any way with the other in connection with Programs in the State of California during the life of the Joint Venture and for one year thereafter.

6. Promptly after the formation of the Company, its authorized representative shall sign a copy of this Agreement, the distribution agreement, and the subdistribution agreement.

7. This Agreement shall terminate upon the dissolution or liquidation of the Company or at such other time as the parties in writing may mutually agree upon. At such time, assets will be distributed equally after payment of Company debts, if any.

8. This agreement may not be assigned to any third party without the permission of all parties.

9. This agreement (together with the forms of distribution agreement and subdistribution agreement attached) shall constitute the entire agreement of the parties with regard to the subject matter and may not be amended without the written consent of all parties.

10. This agreement shall be governed by the laws of the State of California.

The Laura Little Studio, Inc.

By:_____

XYZ Designs

By:_____

EXHIBIT 5

Employment Agreement

Employment Agreement

AGREEMENT made this _____ day of _____ 19___, by and between The Laura Little Studio, Inc. (the "Company') and Andrea Dunn ("Employee").

1. Dunn shall join Company as administrator with a function focus in the area of home office and general office administration.

2. As consideration for your administrative efforts for the company in organizing and administering the Company, Dunn shall be granted an option to purchase 50 shares of Company stock (1%) for $5,000 exercisable at any time after one year from date hereof if she is still associated in a professional capacity with the company.

3. Dunn shall be compensated for her administrative duties at the annual rate of $20,000 commencing as of this date. The salary shall be reviewed by Company no less than annually with a view to increases if that is financially possible for the Company.

4. Dunn shall also be entitled to a commission on revenue to Company obtained through her efforts equal to five percent of the gross revenues to the Company. Commission shall be in addition to salary referred to above.

5. Commission shall apply to original and repeat business from any client introduced by Dunn except that: (a) she must still remain associated with Company and (b) agree to share commission with any other Company personnel who assisted in obtaining said repeat business.

6. Dunn shall be reimbursed for all agreed reasonable business expenses incurred in connection with this agreement.

7. Dunn shall be entitled during the term of her employment to receive such benefits as are available to other employees of like status.

8. Dunn agrees that any material designated by Company as confidential or trade secret material shall be retained as such by Dunn. At the termination of this agreement for any reason, Dunn agrees to return any trade secret or confidential material immediately.

9. It is understood that this agreement requires Dunn's full-time efforts; that Dunn is not an hourly employee and Dunn agrees to devote such time and attention to Company business as reasonably required and agrees not to conflict with the interests of Company and not to compete with the business of Company during her association with the Company and for one year thereafter in the Southeastern United States.

10. Unless terminated earlier for cause, this agreement shall be for an initial term of two years. It may be renewed by Company on 60 days prior notice to Dunn.

11. Until such time as this agreement is superseded, it shall be in full force and effect; it shall not be modified except in writing duly signed; it may not be assigned except by Company to a successor to its business; it shall be governed by the laws of the State.

12. Any disagreement under this agreement shall first be submitted to mediation prior to taking any other action.

Dated and signed at Smallville.

THE LAURA LITTLE STUDIO, INC.

BY; _____
President

_____
Andrea Dunn (Employee)

EXHIBIT 6

Simple Form for Independent Contractor

The XYZ Company, Main Street, USA (called "Company") and independent contractor: _____ (called "Contractor"), agree as follows:

1. The Contractor shall perform certain work for Company as follows: (called the "Work"). Unless specified otherwise, the Work shall remain the property of Company.

2. The Work described above is temporary in nature. Company and Contractor agree that the Work shall be completed in accordance with the following schedule:

3. Time is/is not of the essence of this agreement.

4. Contractor shall be paid for his/her efforts the following sum(s) according to the following schedule:

5. Contractor is not an employee of the Company and shall have no power to act on behalf of the Company except to conduct the following specific tasks as part of this agreement.

6. Contractor is not considered an employee for federal or state tax purposes. Payments made to Contractor in excess of the IRS minimum reportable sum shall be reported to both Contractor and the appropriate tax authorities on IRS Form 1099 (or other form as may be required). It shall be the responsibility of Contractor to assume all tax and individual income reporting obligations relating to his/her fees for this work.

7. Contractor is not considered an employee for insurance or other employee benefits. It shall be the responsibility of Contractor to provide his/her own insurance, hospitalization or other such health or welfare benefits as he/she may require.

8. Certain facilities or equipment may be supplied by the Company to the Contractor as follows. (Said facilities/equipment are provided solely in connection with the Work to be performed under this agreement):

9. Company shall not be liable to Contractor for any injuries or other losses from any cause whatsoever which result from the Work performed hereunder.

10. This is a personal services agreement and may not be assigned by Contractor without the express written consent of Company.

11. This agreement shall be in effect for the period of time required in Paragraph 2 above unless such term is amended or unless either party shall give at least _____ days notice in writing of the intention to terminate the agreement sooner.

12. Contractor agrees to keep confidential any Company information disclosed to him/her of a confidential nature. This provision shall survive this agreement and remain in effect until such information is no longer confidential.

13. This agreement shall be the entire agreement of the parties and may not be changed except in writing.

Dated at _____ this _____ day of _____,19___.

XYZ Company Inc.

By:_____

_____
Contractor

EXHIBIT 7

Promissory Note

Due: January 1, 1996

Promissory Note

Carol Paul Lanyon ("CPL") hereby promises to pay to the order of Ohio Hamburger Systems, Inc. ("OHS") the sum of One thousand dollars ($1,000) on or before June 30, 1996. This note shall bear interest on any unpaid balance at the rate of 12% per annum from the date hereof until payment is made in full.

In the event of nonpayment when due, OHS may take such action as it deems appropriate to collect any sums then due. CPL agrees to pay, in addition to any note balance then due, attorney fees and costs of collection.

This note may be assigned or transferred to a holder in due course.

Notice, presentment and notice of dishonor are hereby waived.

This note shall bind CPL, her heirs, successors and assigns.

Dated at Charlotte this 27th day of March, 1995.

_____
Carol Paul Lanyon

Witness:

_____
Jane Doe

EXHIBIT 8

Bill of Sale

BILL OF SALE

FOR AND IN CONSIDERATION OF THE SUM OF TWO THOUSAND DOLLARS ($2,000) received by me, I hereby sell, convey and assign to Beth Allen ("Buyer") all right, title and interest in the following works of art now owned by me:

1. The Swan—painting by Nathan Emalian.

2. Eros and Eurybia—lithograph by Braque.

I hereby warrant that these works of art are owned by me free and clear of any claim, lien or encumbrance to any third party.

This Bill of Sale is dated at Charlotte, NC this ____ day of August, 1995.

_____
Robert Whalen ("Seller")

EXHIBIT 9

Assignment of Copyright

Assignment of Copyright

For and in consideration of the sum of $10,000 received by me from The Laura Little Group, Inc. ("Group"), I hereby assign and convey forever all right, title and interest in and to a certain software program developed by me known as "Art Studio Program" and copyrighted in my name at the U.S. Copyright Office bearing Registration No._____(the "Copyrighted Software").

Group shall hereafter have any and all rights in and to the Copyrighted Software free and clear of any claim by me or any third person claiming under me.

A copy of this Assignment may be filed with the U.S. Copyright Office at the request of Group and shall serve as notice to all of my assignment of rights.

Dated at Smallville, this _____ day of _____, 1994.

Arthur O. Author

_____
Named Owner of Copyright

EXHIBIT 10

Confidentiality Agreement

For and in consideration of the sum of one dollar and other good and valuable consideration paid to me by Widget Maker Corporation (the "Company"), I hereby agree to keep confidential all material, processes and information which shall be disclosed to me in connection with the Widget Maker Process.

The undertaking in this agreement shall survive in perpetuity unless and until I shall have received permission to disclose such information by Company or such information is disclosed by the Company and that fact shall be made known to me.

Signed at Widgetville, ST this _____ day of _____,1994.

_____

I. B. Wright

Witness:

_____

For Widget Maker Corporation

EXHIBIT 11

Mediation Clause

To be included in an any agreement

The parties agree that any controversy arising out of this agreement or any interpretation of this agreement which they are not able to resolve themselves shall be submitted to mediation before any other legal action is taken. The parties agree that: _____ shall be the mediator (or such other mediator as the parties may agree upon). Costs and expenses of the mediation shall be borne equally by the parties. Mediation shall take place within two weeks after notification by the aggrieved party of a request for mediation unless extended by the mediator. If the mediation does not result in an agreement acceptable to all sides, each may take such other further action as he/she/it deems advisable under law or equity. In the event, any party takes such legal action without first submitting the issue(s) to mediation as required by this clause, the moving party shall pay the legal expenses of the responding party plus all court costs incurred by said action.

Note: This clause may be inserted into existing agreements, by amendment or modification as provided for in the agreement. In new or pending agreements, it may be utilized by giving a copy to counsel with instructions to include this type of clause or placing into the agreement yourself. Since this is a generic clause, it may not be suitable in your individual situation.

EXHIBIT 12

Request To Negotiate

In letter form, to be addressed to the other side of the dispute.

To:

I want you to know that I am committed to ironing out our differences.

I want you to know that I am prepared to do some thinking and re-thinking if that is what it takes to resolve matters with you.

I want you to know that I value our relationship and am confident that we can work this out in a fair and reasonable manner.

I invite you to meet me (talk to me/write to me) to discuss this and I ask only that you bring the same commitment I have to reaching a resolution.

Thank you for considering this request for discussion.

Note: This form can become the basis of a written invitation to communicate as well as of a telephone or personal conversation. If the sincerity and commitment to iron it out can be heard by the other side, they will agree to negotiate.

EXHIBIT 13

Submission Agreement

SUBMISSION AGREEMENT

AGREEMENT entered into as of the _____ day of _____, 19____, between John Doe of Smallville ("Discloser"); and The Laura Little Studio, Inc., a corporation with its principal place of business at 1020 Main Street, Smallville. ("Company").

DISCLOSER has stated to Company that he has developed a cartoon character for consideration for advertising or licensing use (the "Character"); and

COMPANY is in the business of developing, packaging and distributing artwork, advertising and licensed products.

DISCLOSER claims that the Character is proprietary, but he would like to submit the Character in order that Company may consider it for inclusion in its product line.

IT IS AGREED, for good and valuable consideration given and received, and pursuant to the terms, conditions below, as follows:

1.1 Discloser shall disclose certain proprietary information about the design of the Character (the "Information").

1.2 The following shall at no time be considered Information, regardless of whether or not it has been marked "Proprietary":

    (a) information already known to Company;

    (b) information which becomes publicly known through no wrongful or unlawful act;

    (c) information rightfully and lawfully received from a third-party without restriction or breach of any agreement;

(d) information independently developed by Company;

(e) information furnished to any third party by Discloser without restriction on its use, release or publication.

2.1 Discloser shall deliver to Company an executed original of this Agreement and the Information concerning the Character. All Information submitted by Discloser to Company shall remain the property of Discloser.

2.2 Company shall safeguard Information labelled "Proprietary" as if it were Company confidential information; but in no event shall Company be liable, should there be an inadvertent disclosure of such Information, so long as Company had taken reasonable steps to preserve confidentiality, and, upon learning of such disclosure, uses its best efforts to retrieve such Information and to prevent any further inadvertent disclosure.

2.3 In the event Discloser wishes to withdraw the submission from consideration by Company, Discloser shall state that fact in a writing mailed to Company by registered mail, return receipt requested, which letter also gives directions as to the return or destruction of the Information.

3.1 Company shall review the Information submitted by Discloser and shall inform Discloser as soon as possible as to whether Company wishes to enter into an agreement with Discloser with regard to a transfer of rights thereto and the terms of said agreement.

3.2 In the event Company decides not to enter into any further agreement with Discloser, Company shall return the Information provided to it by Discloser by prepaid registered or certified mail, return receipt requested or by delivery of the materials to Discloser at his place of work.

3.3 This Agreement shall not be construed as granting or conferring any rights other than those expressly stated herein except to provide Discloser such protection as he may also have under the patent laws of the United States.

(Exhibit 13 continued on next page)

EXHIBIT 13

(continued)

3.4 This agreement contains all terms of the agreement and may not be amended or modified except in writing duly signed.

3.5. This agreement shall be governed by the laws of the State of Idaho.

The Laura Little Studio, Inc.

_____

_____

Discloser

EXHIBIT 14

(Software) License Agreement

PLEASE READ THIS FIRST!

The XYZ Corporation Software is the property of XYZ Corporation ("XYZ"). This agreement establishes legal rights between XYZ and the User. Users should clearly understand the following specific conditions upon which software is supplied.

1. LICENSE

This software is licensed. XYZ Corporation, Inc. ("XYZ") claims copyrights in the software, screen output and documentation. Legal title to the software remains in XYZ. The software is licensed for support of health-related assessments of individuals, employees, relatives of employees, retired employees, agents and contractors of licensee.

Any use of this software not in accordance with the above conditions constitutes a breach of the license agreement between XYZ and the User and may also constitute a violation of U.S. and other Copyright Laws or other laws, rules or regulations.

2. LIMITED WARRANTY

This software is furnished by XYZ under the following Limited Warranty: XYZ warrants that the Program disks supplied in connection with this software are free from defects in materials and workmanship, assuming normal use, for a period of 90 days from date of acquisition by User. If a defect occurs during this period, the User may return the faulty disk to XYZ with a record of the Acquisition Date. XYZ will replace the defective disk free of charge. For other problems and User Support, see the Manual.

(Exhibit 14 continued on next page)

EXHIBIT 14

(continued)

NOTICE

EXCEPT FOR THE LIMITED EXPRESS WARRANTY SET FORTH
ABOVE, XYZ Corporation, Inc. GRANTS NO OTHER WARRANTIES,
EXPRESS OR IMPLIED, BY STATUTE OR OTHERWISE, REGARDING
THE DISKS AND UNDERLYING SOFTWARE AND RELATED MATERI-
ALS, THEIR FITNESS FOR ANY PURPOSE, THEIR QUALITY, THEIR
MERCHANTABILITY OR OTHERWISE. THE LIABILITY OF XYZ
Corporation, Inc. UNDER THE WARRANTY SET FORTH ABOVE
SHALL BE LIMITED TO THE AMOUNT PAID BY USER FOR RIGHT
TO USE THE PRODUCT. IN NO EVENT SHALL XYZ Corporation,
Inc. BE LIABLE FOR ANY SPECIAL, CONSEQUENTIAL OR OTHER
DAMAGES FOR BREACH OF WARRANTY.

3. TRADEMARK NOTICE

The trademarks: "XYZ-Software" and "The Chips Games" are trademarks of XYZ Corporation, Inc.

EXHIBIT 15

Company Dispute Resolution Policy

Subject: <u>Alternative Dispute Resolution</u>

This organization recognizes that for many business disputes there is a less expensive, easier to handle, more effective method of resolution than the traditional legal process. Alternative Dispute Resolution (ADR) procedures involve techniques which can often spare businesses the high cost and adverse impact of litigation.

In recognition of the foregoing, this firm subscribes to the following statement of principle on behalf of our company and its subsidiaries:

> In the event of a business dispute between our company and another company, we are committed to exploring with that other party resolution of the dispute through direct negotiation or ADR techniques in good faith before pursuing full-scale litigation. If either our company or the other party believes that the dispute is not suitable for ADR techniques, or if such techniques do not produce results satisfactory to the disputants, either party may proceed with litigation.

In all relationships both within and without this form, this Policy Statement should be borne in mind.

_____
Chief Executive Officer

_____
Date

Source: Based upon a proposal to companies by the Center for Public Resources (CPR). 680 Fifth Avenue, New York, New York 10019.

Note: If your firm executes a policy similar to this one, a copy of the policy statement may be sent to CPR at the address above and/or to Mediate-Tech, Inc. P.O. Box 375, Charlottesville, VA 22902; both maintain registries of companies that have agreed to resolve disputes through ADR and provide dispute resolvers.

APPENDIX II
RESOURCES

Development emphasizes the need of extensive and personal acquaintance with a small number of typical situations with a view to mastering the way of dealing with the problems of experience, not the piling up of information.

—Rousseau

WHOM TO CONTACT

In most areas, the first place to look for assistance with a legal problem is a licensed, professional attorney.

If you do not already have one, the best way to find an attorney is to be referred to a qualified professional, experienced in your field of business or in commercial law; any successful business or professional person will have had dealings with an attorney.

If you do not know anyone to ask, consult the local bar association. In most urban areas, you will find a state bar association, a county association and local associations. Nationally, the American Bar Association's specialty sections include business and commercial law. Any of these associations will probably have a legal referral service that functions in a professional, nonbiased manner, designed to give you the name of an attorney who is experienced in your area of interest.

If you live in or near a college or university, contact the law school—if they have one—or the business or commercial department for the name of an attorney experienced in business. Often, especially at community colleges, an adjunct member of the faculty who is a practicing attorney can help; just beware of the novice.

Since advertising is now permitted for lawyers, you might try looking for a lawyer in the telephone company's *Yellow Pages*. Some attorneys are permitted by their local rules to list the fields in which they practice. Check to see whether the listing implies special knowledge or qualifications in your specialty field. Most bar associations require lawyers who advertise specialties to be specially qualified or to use warning words that they are only claiming an interest in a particular field.

If you are bogged down in a problem or dispute and feel that you and the other side could benefit from some solid facilitation before you both dash to attorneys, give serious thought to professional mediation. To find a mediator, look under "Mediation" in the telephone company's *Yellow Pages*. Some phone books list mediators under "Arbitration and Mediation."

Mediators may be available from either public—nonprofit—sources or private practitioners. Ask the person you call whether he or she is experienced in the domain of your dispute; if not, ask for a recommendation to someone who is. Be sure also to ask how much they charge and whether or not they are available for one-on-one consulting if you should need that; while some mediators will do that, others will not.

Mediation is a growing professional field and includes people who have just been trained or have unilaterally proclaimed themselves qualified. At this time, few states regulate mediators. Take care to ascertain the background and level of training of anyone you call for help.

If you cannot find someone in your community, ask an attorney about the names of members of the ADR Committee of the Bar Association. If you still cannot locate a mediator, there are several centralized listings. Listed below are names and phone numbers of several organizations that can help you find a mediator.

Society of Professionals in Dispute Resolution (SPIDR)

Membership organization for mediation professionals
202 783-7277

The American Bar Association Standing Committee on Dispute Resolution

Maintains a clearing house of firms, organizations and individuals and publishes an annual directory of ADR providers
202 331-2258

Bureau of National Affairs

Private Information and publishing firm that maintains a list of providers, which can be purchased   800 452-7773

Academy of Family Mediators

Professional membership organization of divorce and family mediators   503 345-1205

National Association of Mediators in Education

Membership group of mediators involved with education
413 545-2462

Harvard Negotiation Project

Publishes <u>Consensus</u> and maintains a comprehensive list of public and private conflict resolution providers
617 495-1684

RESOURCES FOR FURTHER READING

There are a number of very good and easy-to-read books about business law. If you are serious about the subject, many larger urban libraries, most university libraries, almost all courthouses and all law schools have law libraries. Here, you can find law books and journals on virtually every topic of law.

You can usually also find a terminal for one or both of the two popular on-line data information systems available to lawyers, judges and students in the United States: *Lexis* from Mead Data Central and *Westlaw* from West Publishing Company. Lexis and Westlaw contain most recent law cases, state and federal statutes and other legal research resources. A librarian or a law student may be able to help you search these systems.

The following books will expand your knowledge of business law and ADR:

American Bar Association. *You and the Law*. American Bar Association, Chicago, 1991.
A general guide in question and answer format. It contains some very good, however brief, information on business law topics.

Anderson. *Business Law*. eleventh edition. Cincinnati, Ohio: South-Western Publishing Co., 1980.
Textbook that covers all the basics. Look for a later edition.

Barnes, Dworkin and Richards, *Law for Business Third Edition*. Homewood, IL: Richard D. Irwin, Inc., 1987.
Excellent student text.

Burton, and Dukes. *Conflict Practices in Management, Settlement and Resolution*. New York: St. Martin's Press, 1990.
About the dispute resolution process; part of an excellent series.

Dungan, and Ridings. *Business Law*. New York: Barrons, 1990.
Part of the Barron's Business Library, this book is recommended highly. Watch the date; legal information can quickly become stale when laws and late decisions change.

Folberg, and Taylor. *Mediation: A Comprehensive Guide to Resolving Conflict Without Litigation*. San Francisco: Jossey-Bass, 1984
Good introduction to the dispute resolution process.

Goldberg, Green and Sander. *Dispute Resolution*. Boston: Little Brown, 1985.
One of the most widely accepted introductions to the dispute resolution process.

Keltner. *Mediation: Toward a Civilized System of Dispute Resolution*. Annandale, VA: Speech Communication Association, 1987.
One of the best small books available on mediation.

Kling. *The Complete Guide to Everyday Law*. New York: Berkley Publishing Group, 1983.
  Very popular general guide with some valuable data and forms. Look for a later edition if one is available.

Lickson. *Ironing It Out: Seven Simple Steps to Resolving Conflicts*. Charlottesville, VA: MLM Publishing, 1993.
  Basic primer on conflict and self-resolution; includes good resources section.

Lovenheim. *Mediate Don't Litigate*. New York: McGraw-Hill, 1990.
  Deservedly popular book on the field of mediation.

Moore. *The Mediation Process: Practical Strategies for Resolving Conflict*. San Francisco: Jossey-Bass, 1986.
  Written by one of the better known mediators and trainers in the United States.

Prentice Hall Editorial Staff. *Lawyer's Desk Book*. Englewood Cliffs, NJ: Prentice Hall, 1989.
  Latest in a series of books prepared as desk guides for practicing lawyers. Very comprehensive but limited in topics. Prentice Hall will be coming out with a new edition in the near future.

Singer. *Settling Disputes: Conflict Resolution in Business, Families and the Legal System*. Boulder, CO: Westview Press, 1990.
  Introduces ADR and looks at directions of development of the field.

GLOSSARY

ACCEPTANCE
The indication of willingness to enter into a contract.

ACCORD
An agreement.

ACKNOWLEDGMENT
Agreeing before an officer who can take an oath.

ACTION
A formal legal proceeding.

ADR
Alternative Dispute Resolution. This is the generally accepted term in the law and professional dispute resolution community.

ADJUDICATION
The process of going forward in the traditional court system to obtain a judgment on the merits of an issue.

AGREEMENT
The outcome of a successful discussion, negotiation or other process that represents the meeting of the minds of the parties with respect to the subject matter. It may be oral or in writing and is usually binding unless expressed otherwise.

ARBITRATION
The process whereby a neutral third person is designated by parties in a dispute to hear the issue and render a decision. The parties may decide in advance whether or not that decision will be binding. Arbitration is considered an ADR procedure.

ASSIGN
To transfer some interest in something.

AWARD
The outcome of an arbitration.

BAILMENT

A delivery of goods under an agreement that the goods be cared for reasonably by the bailee—one who receives the goods.

BANKRUPTCY

(1) A formal proceeding whereby debtor seeks discharge or release from certain debts; (2) Failure to meet current obligations when due or liabilities exceeding assets.

BILL OF LADING

Both a receipt and a contract by a common carrier that goods have been received for shipment.

BINDING

The agreement of the parties to give full legal effect to their outcome.

BREACH

Breaking a law or regulation or any duty. Violation of a contract.

CAVEAT EMPTOR

Latin term for "let the buyer beware."

CHECK

Written instructions or order to a bank to pay.

COLLATERAL

Goods pledged to secure a debt.

COMMON LAW

The body of law upon which the Anglo-American legal system is based, reflecting court-recognized legal theories and precedents.

COMPROMISE

The midpoint between two competing positions.

CONCILIATION

The process where a neutral assists parties in resolving a dispute by direct discussion, with each usually not in the presence of the others.

CONFLICT
Any disagreement or dispute or other issue that forces a choice upon the person.

CONFLICT OF LAWS
The conflict of laws between two or more legal entities—i.e., states or countries.

CONSENT
Alignment of thinking on some issue; agreement.

CONSIDERATION
The thing of value exchanged that makes a contract valid.

CONSTRUCTIVE NOTICE
A legal term implying notice from the facts and actions of the parties.

CONTRACT
A legally binding, mutual undertaking.

COUNSELING
The process conducted by a fully qualified and licensed professional—e.g., attorney or mental health provider—designed to assist the party or parties with their situation.

CONVEY
To formally transfer title.

COURT
A place designated by the state to officially hear disputes between and among parties; presided over by a judge.

DAMAGE
A loss suffered by a party, to a person or property.

DECLARATORY JUDGMENT
An action seeking a court to define parties' rights or duties toward something.

DECREE
The judgment or pronouncement of the court.

DEED

A document transferring title (usually to real estate); must be executed in a formalized manner described by statute.

DEFAMATION

A tort, the act of damaging a person's reputation either orally or in writing.

DEFAULT

An unwillingness or inability to live up to a legal obligation.

DEFENDANT

The party against whom a formal legal action has been initiated by the plaintiff.

DEPOSITION

Testimony taken by one or more parties outside the tribunal before an officer empowered to administer oaths.

DISCHARGE

A legal release or completion of an obligation.

DISPUTANTS

The parties who are engaged in a process to resolve their dispute.

ENDORSE

The act by which a negotiable instrument is passed along; i.e., writing one's name on back of a check or draft.

EQUITY

A system that serves as an auxiliary to the law—available in a court of law—to prevent injustice in civil matters.

ESCROW

Turning over something of value to a third party, who acts as an agent for the parties to hold the money or goods until certain conditions are met.

FACILITATION

A general term used whenever a third party assists others in reaching mutually established goals.

FIDUCIARY
A person or organization in a special trust relationship with another.

GRANT
The passage of something from one to another.

GUARANTOR
A person who serves as surety for another.

IMPASSE
That point in a discussion, negotiation or mediation where it becomes apparent that parties are unwilling or unable to come to agreement.

INDEMNITY
To secure a person or firm against loss.

INJUNCTION
An order of the equity court prohibiting someone from doing something or mandating them to do something.

JUDGMENT
A final, binding, order of court; the outcome of legal proceedings.

LACHES
Undue delays in taking some action.

LIEN
A right asserted against or upon something allowing possession until the obligation underlying it is satisfied.

MEDIATION
The process whereby a neutral third party, selected by the disputants, assists them in reaching accord through distinct procedural steps designed to develop agreement. The parties set the ground rules and may agree to be bound or not.

MISREPRESENTATION
The intentional misstatement of present facts designed to induce someone to do something.

MORTGAGE
A conveyance of legal title to property—usually land—to serve as collateral for a debt.

NEGLIGENCE
A tort action; the failure to live up to a duty, causing injury and damages. Must be proximately connected to the alleged misconduct.

NEGOTIABLE
The aspect of a financial instrument that allows it to freely pass in commerce.

NEGOTIATION
The act of passing along a negotiable instrument. Also a term used to describe active and committed discussion designed to reach specific goals.

NOTE
A written promise to pay money.

OMBUDSPERSON
A person usually designated by an organization to function in a so-called neutral capacity to assist people dealing with that organization.

PLAINTIFF
The person who initiates a formal legal action against a defendant.

PLEADINGS
The documents filed with the court to establish jurisdiction and other aspects of a case.

PLEDGE
A promise signified by the giving of goods as security.

POWER OF ATTORNEY
Assignment to another of legal power to undertake specified activity on behalf of the assignor.

PRIVATE OR RENT-A-JUDGE
The process of hiring a person—usually a retired judge—to hear a dispute; most often these result in arbitrations.

PUBLIC DISPUTE
A dispute or problem that directly or indirectly affects a large group, community or segment of society.

QUASI-CONTRACT
An implied contract, created by the acts of the parties.

ROYALTY
The agreed payment to a licensor or grantor of rights to sell, publish or otherwise use one's rights.

SETTLEMENT
An agreement that represents the successful outcome of a discussion, negotiation or ADR process, and that ends the dispute.

SPECIFIC PERFORMANCE
The order of court to parties to perform the contract as written.

STATUTE OF LIMITATIONS
The time limits set by the legislature within which certain actions may be brought to the courts.

SUIT
The action in the courts.

SUMMARY JUDGMENT
A method by which a party asks for a decision, based on the pleadings alone, assuming all facts in the pleadings are correct.

SUMMONS
A call to the court; used to begin a legal action or to obtain the presence of a party at court.

TERM

The length of running of a contract.

TORT

An actionable, noncontract legal wrong.

TRUST

The basis for special reliance; also a form by which something is held for the benefit of someone else.

TRUSTEE

A fiduciary who is asked to administer a trust for the benefit of another.

USURY

An unlawfully high rate of interest.

VOID

Of absolutely no legal force or effect.

VOIDABLE

May result in no legal effect if asserted.

WARRANTY

A special undertaking in an agreement.

WRIT

A judicial instrument by which an action goes forth; see also summons.

ABOUT THE AUTHOR

Charles P. Lickson graduated from John Hopkins University and Georgetown Law Center. Following 15 years of law practice, Mr. Lickson entered the business field and founded the *Computer User's Legal Reporter,* a newsletter on law/technology topics. He is currently president of Mediate-Tech, Inc., specializing in the field of alternative dispute resolution. He is certified in Commercial, Divorce and Technical Mediation and consults with state and federal government, companies and individuals on conflict management and resolution. His publications include *Computers and the Law: Workbook and Materials,* Conflict and Mediation Skills and *Ethics for Government Employees.*

NOTES

NOTES

NOTES

NOTES

NOTES

NOTES

ABOUT CRISP PUBLICATIONS

We hope that you enjoyed this book. If so, we have good news for you. This title is only one in the library of Crisp's best-selling books. Each of our books is easy to use and is obtainable at a very reasonable price.

Books are available from your distributor. A free catalog is available upon request from Crisp Publications, Inc., 1200 Hamilton Court, Menlo Park, California 94025. Phone: (415) 323-6100; Fax: (415) 323-5800.

Books are organized by general subject area.

Computer Series
Beginning DOS for Nontechnical Business Users	212-7
Beginning Lotus 1-2-3 for Nontechnical Business Users	213-5
Beginning Excel for Nontechnical Business Users	215-1
DOS for WordPerfect Users	216-X
WordPerfect Styles Made Easy	217-8
WordPerfect Sorting Made Easy	218-6
Getting Creative with Newsletters in WordPerfect	219-4
Beginning WordPerfect 5.1 for Nontechnical Business Users	214-3

Management Training
Building a Total Quality Culture	176-7
Desktop Design	001-9
Ethics in Business	69-6
Ethics for Government Employees	208-9
Formatting Letters and Memos	130-9
From Technician to Supervisor	194-5
Goals and Goal Setting	183-X
Increasing Employee Productivity	010-8
Introduction to Microcomputers	087-6
Leadership Skills for Women	62-9
Managing for Commitment	099-X
Managing Organizational Change	80-7
Motivating at Work	201-1
Quality at Work	72-6
Systematic Problem Solving and Decision Making	63-2
21st Century Leader	191-0

Personal Improvement

Communications

Small Business and Financial Planning